# Cross Creek Kitchens

# Cross Creek

## Seasonal Recipes and Reflections

By Sally Morrison

Illustrations by Kate Barnes

TRIAD PUBLISHING COMPANY   GAINESVILLE, FLORIDA

# Kitchens

*Cross Creek Kitchens is available at special quantity discounts for bulk purchases for sales promotions, premiums, or fund raising. For details write the Director of Special Sales, Triad Publishing Company, 1110 Northwest Eighth Avenue, Gainesville, Florida 32601.*

**Library of Congress Cataloging in Publication Data**

Morrison, Sally, 1949-
Cross Creek kitchens

Includes index.
1. Cookery, American — Florida.   2. Cross Creek (Fla.)
— Social life and customs.   3. Rawlings, Marjorie, Kinnan,
1896-1953. I. Title.
TX715.M86055   1983   641.59759   83-5117
ISBN 0-937404-50-0 (hard)
ISBN 0-937404-06-3 (pbk.)

Published and distributed by Triad Publishing Company, Inc.
1110 Northwest Eighth Avenue, Gainesville, Florida 32601

# Foreword

Dear Friends:

As Governor and First Lady of Florida, we are happy to welcome you to the unique culinary and artistic delights of CROSS CREEK KITCHENS. Sally Morrison and Kate Barnes have collaborated to create a book that not only passes on marvelous seasonal recipes from North and Central Florida, but that also provides the reader and user with a feeling for the passage of time in this beautiful section of our State.

Floridians are justly proud of the sunny beaches and cosmopolitan city life for which our State is perhaps most famous. CROSS CREEK KITCHENS adds to this picture the pleasures of life in the rural interior areas where many of our State's pioneer families settled. This book is, in a way, a tribute to their way of life and their appreciation of the wonderful land they called home.

With warm regards,

Sincerely,

Governor

First Lady

June 13, 1983

# Prologue

The village of Cross Creek is on an isthmus between two large lakes. In this locale, Spaniards once planted orange groves and Indians enjoyed an abundance of readily-available foods. Early settlers lived off the land — farming, fishing, and tending citrus groves.

Marjorie Kinnan Rawlings, one of Florida's most famous authors, moved from the city to this secluded area in Florida's interior in 1928 to create a simpler, happier life for herself. Here, she immortalized the culture of her backwoods neighbors in such classics as *Cross Creek*, *South Moon Under*, and her Pulitzer Prize winner, *The Yearling*.

Her home at Cross Creek is now a state historic site. As tour guide for the Florida Park Service, I once lived in the Rawlings farmhouse, and today I still cook and garden there to show visitors what rural Florida was like fifty years ago. As I tend the woodstove in the Rawlings kitchen, I listen to their responses. People long for the tranquility and serenity they find here. The fragrance of wood smoke and bread baking attracts visitors to the kitchen and seems to summon up a yearning for a less hurried life and for the incomparable taste of fresh food. Many eye the garden wistfully, envious not only of its yield, but also of the self-sufficiency and independence it provides. Some plead to buy the home-canned goods in the pantry, though they are not for sale. Others want to take home the sweet potatoes with sand still clinging to the skins or to pick oranges from the trees.

While living at the Rawlings house, I made friends with my neighbor, watercolor artist Kate Barnes. Our friendship began, appropriately enough, with an exchange of homemade breads. Before long, we were swapping garden vegetables, homemade jams, and original recipes. A friend suggested, half-seriously, that we set up a roadside stand and go into business selling produce, pies, and preserves. But that was not what Kate and I had in mind.

Instead, the two of us decided to share our fondness for life at Cross Creek and of "cooking with the seasons" through this cookbook. Kate and I created our recipes for *Cross Creek Kitchens* in three Florida kitchens — in mine, surrounded by orange groves and gardens, in Kate's at her century-old, historic "Grove House," and in the old-fashioned kitchen of Marjorie Kinnan Rawlings' farmhouse.

Forty years ago, Marjorie Kinnan Rawlings wrote her own cookbook, *Cross Creek Cookery*, which has long influenced my southern cooking. However, Marjorie's cookbook emphasized "company fare — on the rich side and not recommended for daily consumption." Aware of the modern inclination for low-calorie, natural foods, we offer this lighter, more contemporary version of Florida country cooking as a companion to the earlier regional classic.

*Sally Morrison*
*September, 1983*

# Contents

# Recipe Contents

## Salads

## Salad Dressings

## Soups

# Breads

# Main Dishes

# Side Dishes

# Beverages

# Fish and Seafood

# Breakfasts and Brunches

# Desserts

# Pickles and Relishes

# Jams, Preserves and Syrups

# Sauces, Butters and Vinegars

# Part One
# Our Cross Creek Kitchens

# 1. The Red-Birds Do

Sunlight slants through the screens leaving shadows across the floor. The smooth wood boards feel cool to my bare feet as I sweep sand out the porch door. Except for an occasional board creaking, the house is quiet and a morning mist covers the windows. Outside, red-birds come to the feed basket in the crepe myrtle just as they did fifty years ago when Marjorie Kinnan Rawlings lived here. Cross Creek in those days was a fishing village named for the cypress-lined creek that flowed from Lochloosa Lake to Orange Lake. The village gave its name to a book, Marjorie Rawlings' humorous and poignant tale of Cross Creek life, in the 1930s.

Marjorie Rawlings was a vigorous, insightful, determined woman who could make the most ordinary events seem interesting and, often, quite funny. She gave up northern city life and bought a seventy-two acre citrus farm in north Florida, where she developed a profound respect for the pride and intelligence of her rural "cracker" neighbors and a reverence for the area's wild, exotic beauty. Attached though she was to her groves, farm, and home, she trusted time as arbiter of her property. In the last chapter of *Cross Creek* she pondered, "Who owns Cross Creek?" and answered in the same breath, "The red-birds, I think . . . ."

Today the descendents of those red-birds continue to build their nests in the orange grove. As I watch them this morning, I'm reassured by a sense of continuity. Nearly a half century has passed since Marjorie Rawlings introduced Cross Creek to the world. Times have changed. The community is growing. Yet residents continue to cherish the serenity and beauty of this still-rural section of north central Florida. The creek, though altered, still flows steadily from lake to lake. The seasons continue their cyclic pattern.

When I was a child growing up in Florida, my dad gave me a copy of *Cross Creek*. I never expected years later to be resident park ranger and caretaker at the historic Cross Creek farmhouse. My quick acceptance of the park ranger position hadn't given me time to find a place to live, so that when I arrived for work the first day my car was still packed with suitcases, boxes, a tent, and some cooking utensils. My supervisor assessed the situation and arranged for me to live in the Rawlings house until I could find a place of my own. What better way to learn about Marjorie Rawlings' life and home than to live right there immersed in it?

The 100-year-old farmhouse was a museum when I moved in. It had not been lived in for many years and was no longer functional as a home. It was stiff and formal. There were ribbons across the furniture and DO NOT USE signs scattered about the house. There was no hot water, the wood cookstove in the kitchen didn't work, and the old-fashioned icebox required seventy-five-pound blocks of ice. Yet with a slow inevitability, as the house was lived in, it became a home again.

I spent each day as tour guide for tourists and locals, avid
Rawlings fans and those who had never heard of *The Yearling.*
Every morning before 9 a.m., my pillow and toothbrush, my banjo
and books had to be stuffed in the closet away from public
scrutiny. I made sure to take my cold bath before the first visitor
arrived. Often the house was filled with talk and laughter as a
steady stream of people toured the house. The screen doors
slammed, the pitcher pump creaked, footsteps resounded along
wooden floors.

# Grapefruit Biscuits

½ cup whole wheat pastry flour, sifted
1½ cups unbleached white flour, sifted
½ teaspoon baking soda
½ teaspoon salt
1 teaspoon baking powder
½ teaspoon nutmeg (optional)
3 tablespoons butter
⅓ cup grapefruit juice, combined with
⅓ cup water

Preheat oven to 475°. Sift together flour, baking soda, salt, and baking powder. Mix in butter lightly with finger tips until the mixture has the consistency of coarse cornmeal. Make a well in the center and add grapefruit and water mixture while stirring.

Knead gently a few times on lightly floured board, adding a little flour or grapefruit juice if necessary. Pat the dough to ½-inch thickness and cut with floured biscuit cutter.

Place on greased baking sheet and bake in 475° oven for about 3 minutes. Turn heat down to 400° and bake until done (approximately another 10 minutes).

Makes 10 to 12 biscuits.

Note: Juice from sour oranges may be used instead of grapefruit.

After visiting hours, the house and I lapsed into welcome silence. Occasionally I heard the soft thumping of wood floorboards as the old house settled a little into the sand. Young boys walking the road sometimes called a greeting as I played my banjo on the porch. At night the mellow glow of indirect lighting — cast by wooden bowls covering bare bulbs — reflected on the high ceilings. Evening breezes sighed over the shingled roof and through the open breezeways. With its airy porches and numerous doors and windows, the house imposed little barrier between inside and outdoors. A frog chorus resounded from nearby woods, and barred owls called to each other. Late at night, I'd awaken to a distant train sounding its drawn-out chord across Lochloosa marsh.

There was a certain ease to living in the old farmhouse even though facilities were minimal. As the red-birds sang awaiting their feed each morning, I'd watch the sun rise through the orange trees. I soon discovered that I could walk to the lake's edge to pick a simple breakfast of ripe blackberries. In the abandoned citrus grove, I found the last of winter's grapefruit, especially sweet for the long maturing. When I'd get a hankering for a hot meal, I'd cook fresh bass over an outdoor fire. Drawing up a palm log to sit on, I'd wait until hoe cake and sweet potatoes finished baking in the coals. As the clouds cleared from the sky, the stars brightened and the night air turned as crisp as the cornmeal breading on the fish. The spicy scent of magnolia blooms filled the spring night. I savored the moment as much as the food.

# Orange Blossom Carrot Cake

2 cups unbleached white flour
1 teaspoon baking powder
½ teaspoon baking soda
½ teaspoon cinnamon
½ teaspoon nutmeg
2 teaspoons grated orange rind
2 cups grated carrots
½ cup raisins
½ cup chopped walnuts or pecans
1 egg, beaten
½ cup orange juice
½ cup orange blossom honey
½ cup plain yogurt

*Frosting*
4 tablespoons butter
2 teaspoons grated orange rind
1½ cups confectioners sugar, sifted
1 tablespoon orange juice

Preheat oven to 350°. In a medium bowl, sift together flour, baking powder, baking soda, and spices. Mix in the orange rind, grated carrot, raisins, and nuts. In a small bowl, mix egg, orange juice, honey, and yogurt and beat well. Add wet ingredients to dry and beat with a spoon until well mixed, about 1 minute.

Pour into a greased 9 x 14 x 2 pan and bake at 350° for 35 minutes or until a knife inserted in center comes out clean. Cool thoroughly.

In a small bowl, soften butter with a wooden spoon and mix in orange rind until well blended and creamy. Add confectioners sugar a little at a time, beating well, until frosting is thick. Add orange juice and beat well. If frosting is too thin, add more sugar. Spread over cooled cake.

Serves 12.

I can't really remember when it began — perhaps with the smell of fresh-squeezed orange juice in the kitchen or with a bouquet of roses on the breakfast table, or when I inadvertently vacuumed the pink ribbons off the red "fainting couch." The other ribbons proved unnecessary and the DO NOT USE signs were put away. The formality of a museum didn't belong here where a woman's life and love and laughter were so rich. I set Marjorie's old typewriter on the front porch table in view of the red-birds' feeder. Seeing an empty coffee cup and the deerhide chair pushed back, visitors paused and asked, "Is she still living here?" Maybe she's gone to pick some roses or refill her coffee cup.

As spring turned into summer, I became eager to plant a garden, both for myself and because gardening had been an integral part of Marjorie's life on the farm. Thirty years had passed since Marjorie's death, however, and there was no sign of the original garden site. In answer to my inquiries, long-time friends of Marjorie's stopped by to point out her garden's backyard location near a chicken coop. The soil now nourished a well-established lawn and had not been turned in years, so that hand-shoveling was difficult. A southern magnolia had sprouted in the abandoned garden spot. I planted around it. Before long I was picking fresh salad greens and washing them in the iron-y water of the pitcher pump. Okra grew to be six feet tall in the rich soil and colorful zinnias accented lush vegetables and herbs.

# Lemon Okra

*I'm grateful to my friend Michael for his unique recipe for lemon okra. I distinctly remember his lavish use of garlic, butter, and lemon, which blended gently with the okra. But when I mentioned the dish to him recently, his response was, "Gee, that sounds good. When are you going to make it?"*

¼ cup butter
2 cloves garlic, minced
4 cups okra, sliced in ½-inch rounds
¼ cup lemon juice
½ teaspoon black pepper
Salt to taste

Melt butter in 10-inch skillet. Add garlic and cook briefly on low heat. Turn heat to medium and cook okra briefly on both sides. Add lemon juice and sprinkle with black pepper and salt to taste. Cover and steam until tender. Serve over brown rice.

Serves 4.

My next project was to begin restoring the farm. I made a trip home, some 150 miles south, and brought back my old Irish setter, Red, and a few chickens I had raised. Traveling late at night to avoid the summer heat, my '58 Chevy chugged through the rolling hills of Florida's central ridge. The back seat was cluttered with crates of restless chickens and a sleeping dog. The next morning my co-worker was surprised by chickens in the pen and a dog in

the yard. Dogs weren't generally allowed in state parks, but I used the convincing tactic that "Marge had one," and this later worked for keeping a cat, too. Now in the mornings I am greeted by the combined clucking of chickens and the clamorous quacking of mallard ducks awaiting their feed; by flowers, vegetables, and herbs still wet with dew; by an old hound lying in the sand and a cat curled on the porch.

# Jane's Lemon Chicken Soup

2 to 3 pound frying chicken
1 small onion, diced
2 or 3 carrots, sliced
2 cups chopped celery
¼ teaspoon pepper
½ teaspoon salt
1½ cups noodles (optional)
2 egg yolks
Juice of ½ lemon
1 tablespoon grated lemon peel

Place chicken in a soup kettle with cold water to cover. Bring to a boil and skim off foam. Add vegetables and seasonings, cover, and simmer for approximately 1½ hours or until tender. Remove chicken. Place noodles in stock and cook until done. Remove pot from heat and let the stock cool down.

Beat egg yolks until light. Add lemon juice and rind and whip until frothy. Take one cup of cool stock and add it slowly to the egg mixture, stirring all the while. (If the stock is too hot, the mixture will curdle.)

Add the egg and lemon mixture to the pot of soup and stir. Cut chicken in bite-size pieces and add to the soup. Gently heat (do not boil).

Fall seemed the ideal time to put the kitchen into working order. The fact that Marjorie's culinary talents were as highly esteemed as her literary ability was reason enough for making her woodstove functional again. My own desire for hot breads and meals was further incentive. Concerned with the fire hazard in an all-wood house, I cleaned the stove, bought new stove pipe, and had the chimney repaired.

Fortunately I had cooked on a woodstove before. I remembered the skills taught to me by my good friend Jane when I lived out West. I began filling the empty jars in the pantry with the seasonal bounty of fruits and vegetables. Absent for some thirty years, the smells of gingerbread and cornbread spread through the homestead once again.

I spent as much time as I could that first winter working the citrus grove that had once been the main focus of the farm. The old grove that had so enchanted Marjorie Rawlings with its symmetrical beauty was overgrown with sapling oaks and vines. Worse yet, the trees had been cold-damaged and seemed unlikely to survive. The scraggly grove now numbered less than sixty of the original 1600 trees and might wisely be let go, especially since it was on the northernmost boundary for citrus in Florida. The decision to maintain the remnant grove or let it grow into woodlands was hanging in the balance. Yet there really was no question about it. I had to try to bring the grove back. With the encouragement and advice of two of Marjorie's grove caretakers who still lived in the area, I began hoeing the trees and cutting out the vines. That first winter I was rewarded with fruit that was sweet and exceptional.

# 2. Marjorie's Kitchen

As I open the kitchen door of the Rawlings house in the morning, the lingering fragrance of wood smoke greets me. I am sure that I smell sausage frying or biscuits baking. On cool winter days when I bake gingerbread or cornbread, visitors who come to the front door are drawn to the kitchen in no time. I grind coffee beans in the crank grinder on the pantry wall and know that the freshly-brewed coffee will soon be ready.

Tempting jars of wild plum and blueberry jam, tangerine jelly, orange marmalade, and okra pickles line the pantry shelves. There are dark bottles of cane syrup and jars of amber honey. Herbs hang drying from the rafters.

# Kumquat Tangerine Jam

6 cups whole kumquats
6 tangerines
1 lemon
3 cups sugar

Wash kumquats and remove any blemishes with sharp knife. Cut in half and squeeze out seeds. Wash tangerines, cut into eighths and remove seeds. Chop coarsely. Cut lemon into thin slices, then chop into ½-inch pieces.

In a large pot, mix fruit with 2 cups water and bring to boil. Stir and cook over low heat 10 minutes. Remove from heat, cover, and allow to stand 8 to 10 hours to develop pectin.

Return fruit to slow boil and add sugar. Stir and cook over low heat until thickened, about 15 minutes. Follow standard canning process for storage, or make a small batch for immediate use. (Important: contact your county extension office home economist or consult USDA bulletin #56 for complete and safe canning instructions.)

Makes 5 to 6 pints.

On the kitchen work table there are bowls of fresh local fruits and vegetables — glossy eggplants, zucchini, and Florida pears. Baskets of pecans from the fall harvest are stored, waiting to be shelled. In a good citrus year, grapefruit and oranges overflow their containers. Near the woodstove are cast-iron skillets and heavy Dutch ovens, old muffin tins, corn dodger pans, and thick enamel cooking pots.

# Southern Pea Soup

1 cup dried black-eyed peas
2 cups dried split peas
3 lean ham hocks with extra fat
    removed
6 cups water
1 large onion, chopped
2 medium turnips, peeled and diced
2 carrots, peeled and sliced
3 cups collard greens or spinach,
    chopped
2 teaspoons grated lemon peel
⅓ cup lemon juice
1 teaspoon dried thyme
½ teaspoon freshly grated black pepper

Soak black-eyed peas overnight in water to cover.

In a crockpot or large soup pot, place the black-eyed peas, split peas, ham hocks, and water and simmer over lowest heat for 4 to 6 hours or until black-eyed peas are tender. Remove ham hocks.

About ½ hour before serving, place the onion, turnips, and carrots in a medium pot. Cover with water, bring to a boil and cook, covered, for 10 minutes or until vegetables are nearly tender. Add greens, cover again, and continue cooking until tender.

Mix together the vegetables, cooking stock, pea soup, thyme, lemon peel, lemon juice, and pepper. Stir and serve hot.

Makes about 12 servings.

I gather hardwood oak and hickory from nearby, start the fire in the woodstove with resinous fat lighter'd pine, and wait expectantly for the first smoke and the crackling of the fire. Orange and pecan wood from the grove prunings add fragrance and a steady heat. The addition of a little pine makes a quick heat and encourages the hardwoods to burn. As the cast-iron stovetop heats up, the coffee pot begins to steam. Smoke drifts out the chimney and across the yard.

# Cranberry-Orange Bread

1½ cups whole wheat flour
1½ cups unbleached white flour
3 teaspoons baking powder
3 tablespoons grated orange peel
1½ cups fresh cranberries, finely
    chopped
1 cup chopped pecans
¾ cup orange blossom honey
1 egg, beaten
1½ cups orange juice
2 tablespoons oil

Preheat oven to 350°. Into a medium bowl, sift together flours and baking powder. Stir in orange peel, cranberries, and nuts.

In a small bowl, mix honey, egg, orange juice, and oil until well blended. Mix wet and dry ingredients and stir until blended.

Pour into 2 greased 4½ x 8½ bread pans and bake at 350° for 45 minutes or until knife inserted in center comes out clean. Remove from pans and cool on wire racks.

Makes 2 loaves.

The crackling of a wood fire is something special. Orange light dances through the stove's cast-iron cracks and reflects on the walls. The fire and fragrance make visitors nostalgic. Often I hear the claim, "Food tasted better cooked on a woodstove," followed by animated discourse about baked sweet potatoes, Grandma's biscuits, and slow-cooked beans and soups. These comments made me realize that more than flavor has been lost in today's fast-food culture and that there is a longing for good foods and tranquil surroundings.

Older folks gather in the old-fashioned kitchen, swapping stories. I stop talking and listen as the room fills with reminiscing. Debates focus on the "good old days" — were they good times or just hard times? Some people say they'd like to go back because, though life was hard, it seemed less stressful, more meaningful. Others claim they would never give up their dishwashers, disposals, and food processors.

A neighbor observing my life at the Rawlings home commented, "You know, Sally, you'll get by if we have another Depression. You know how to live simply. You know how to can and cook on a woodstove. You'll get by." Funny thing is, I never thought of it as just getting by.

# 3. Sally's Kitchen

When the desire for a place of my own set me to moving from the Rawlings home, I knew that I would never be satisfied with a house that didn't bring the outdoors in. I had learned to appreciate the wide porches and airy breezeways. Since I wanted to stay within the Cross Creek community, however, I made do with what was available and spent the next few years moving from one small cramped house to another. One day my brother Steve returned from searching for bee locations in the area and mentioned casually, "That big old house in the orange grove near Cane Hammock looks empty." It wasn't long before I was moving in.

Orange groves and gardens encircle the house. Throughout the seasons, the breezes swaying the cabbage palms move through its rooms. There is no insulation from the owls calling back and forth or from the frogs singing in their ponds at night. I awake to the elusive call of sandhill cranes flying over the house. I run through the grove, hoping to find them feeding in the hayfield again. Day or night, I can walk the white sand road winding past marshes and pond to Orange Lake. I feel rooted in this patch of Florida sand.

Now rosy sunlight streams into my morning kitchen. Red-birds sing in the pear trees. Steam from the morning's tea curls out of a tall earthenware pitcher. Mint and lemongrass grow within easy reach of the kitchen and, when they are blended for tea, their fragrance becomes part of the summer air. A crock of sourdough starter continues its slow bubbling, taking yeast spores from the air around it, transforming the atmosphere of the place into its own unique taste.

# Pink Sunrise

*One morning I awoke early to the call of sandhill cranes. The sunrise was pink across the hay fields as I picked rosy strawberries for this drink.*

1 cup fresh strawberries
3 cups pink grapefruit juice
1 banana

Mix together in blender until smooth.
Serves 2.

I enjoy having a large combined kitchen and dining room with ample space for friendly companionship and help with cooking preparations. An oak dining table doubles as a handy work space for kneading bread or chopping vegetables. My combination wood-burning and electric range provides me the ease and convenience of electricity at a moment's notice as well as the heat and companionable crackling of a wood fire.

# Orange Marmalade Bread

2 tablespoons yeast
2 tablespoons honey
1 cup warm water
1 cup orange juice
2 eggs, beaten
½ cup oil
½ cup dry skim milk
1 cup orange marmalade
4 cups whole wheat flour
4 cups unbleached white flour

Dissolve yeast and honey in warm water in a large bowl. Allow to stand 10 minutes.

Add orange juice, eggs, oil, milk, and orange marmalade. Stir well. Add three cups of whole wheat flour and beat vigorously until smooth and well-blended. Stir in the remaining flour a little at a time. Turn the dough onto a floured board, cover with bowl, and allow to rest 10 minutes.

Knead the dough until smooth and elastic, about 10 minutes, adding small amount more flour if needed. Place the dough in a large oiled bowl and turn so top is greased. Cover with a towel and set in a warm place to rise until doubled in bulk, about 1 hour.

Punch down the dough, cover and allow to rise again for 1 hour. Form into loaves and place in 2 greased 9 x 5 bread pans. Brush tops with oil, cover, and let rise until doubled in bulk, about 1 hour.

Preheat oven to 350°. Bake for 40 to 60 minutes until brown. The loaves should shrink from the sides of the pan and slip out easily.

Makes 2 loaves.

Outside the kitchen door, the red-birds fly to gourd feeders in the orange trees. Their brilliant red is juxtaposed with the ripening oranges. I usually buy seed packets labeled "Large Gourd Mix" and "Small Gourd Mix" and plant them around the orange trees. The mystery of what each vine will become is so tantalizing that sometimes I think I should stop working and just grow gourds. Through the long summer the gourd vines climb steadily up the orange trees until, reaching the top, they spread out. As the pale green gourds form, they hang heavily among the branches.

This year I grew gourds with morning glories over my chicken coop, transforming it from an unsightly tenement into an object of beauty. The game chickens strut about under their luxuriant shade. Early morning feeding is no longer a chore, for the yellow, white and purple-blue blooms greet my half-open eyes. The gourds grow quickly, and every day I spot another gourd that I hadn't noticed the day before.

I string the gourds along ropes for drying on the porch, safe from late-summer rains; a fine mold mottles each gourd with its own unique design. Once dried and hollowed, the gourds have many uses. Some become bird feeders and homes. When I first tied one in an orange tree outside my kitchen door, the red-birds came to it, but warily. They now sit within, a view on all sides, lingering over a quiet meal. During a rainstorm they find shelter and a snack, and the gourd swirls on its string with the perpetual movements of incoming and outgoing flights. I never anticipated when planting these seeds all that they might become: feeders, homes, planters, scoops, and musical instruments. I never imagined when coming to Cross Creek all that was in store.

# 4. Kate's Kitchen

**W**henever I knock on Kate's porch door at the Grove House, I think of Marjorie Rawlings and old Mr. Brice, alternately talking and lapsing into silence on this same porch. Brice was Marjorie's neighbor within "screaming distance"; his two-story home and barn were part of a productive citrus grove and a focal point in the community.

Today these buildings house Kate's and Gary's painting and pottery studios and are a gathering place for their families and friends. The warmth of Kate's kitchen, with its rich-hued wood counters, the hand-made pottery in all shapes and textures, the ferns, the baskets, and Kate's paintings on the walls, encourages guests to linger long after a meal is finished. Folks bicker good-naturedly over who gets to wash the dishes because dishwashing in Kate's kitchen means a chance to handle the handsome pottery bowls and cups. Occasionally Kate must literally ease someone out the door, apologetically mentioning a neglected painting schedule.

Kate and I put together simple social meals with relative ease. I carry a basket of garden bounty over as an excuse for a little socializing. Kate picks a complementary variety of vegetables from her garden and deftly whips up a batch of muffins or a quick bread. When we set to work creating a new recipe, another seasonal speciality, we feel a conspiratorial triumph. If there is any competition between us, it's of the good-natured variety. Though we take our cooking seriously, our experimentation is somewhat carefree and a recipe changes according to whim or whatever is available. There is no motive to impress — only to enjoy.

## The Long Hungrys

Long before people worried about cholesterol and other dietary menaces, Marjorie Rawlings called her cream and butter laden recipes "utterly deadly." Our recipes are lighter, less rich, but as "utterly" delicious, as attested to by the unwavering faithfulness of the "long hungrys" who hover expectantly near Kate's stove. I found reference to this term in Harry Crews' book, *A Childhood:* "To be long hungry meant you were a glutton, a hog at the trough." Being called a long hungry used to be fighting words.

Today Kate and I use the term to denote endearment, rather than insult. We look upon the long hungrys of our acquaintance with affection, for they show a near reverence for the dedicated cook. They wait patiently for home cooking in preference to the convenience of fast foods. They have in common the appreciation of good food. Our friend Sean is the longest of the long hungrys, and his appetite is as big as his 6'7" frame. He can consume an entire sweet potato pie in one sitting. I've known him to trade his carpentry skills for the promise of a lifetime supply of homemade pies. My beekeeper brother "Sticky" Steve is known for his rallying call, "Don't starve, folks, let's eat!" Starvation is hardly imminent, however, as he cuts one portion of pie and then must even the edges of the remaining pie as an excuse for another piece. Nick doesn't even bother with excuses as he goes back for seconds and thirds, then brazenly blames the grinning cook for his overindulgence. My brother Doug often begins his meal while standing in the kitchen, choosing to stand at the serving counter rather than to sit down. Because of this long-time habit, his own kitchen has been dubbed "Doug's Stand-Up Diner." Gary has perfected the art of hovering near the cooking. He stays in the kitchen, carefully preparing salad dressing, to insure his availability for recipe testing.

# Hogwild Macaroni and Cheese

*This dish is so named because it generally causes the menfolk to lose all control. The addition of herbs to the basic macaroni and cheese makes a new experience out of an old favorite.*

2 cups elbow macaroni, preferably
   whole wheat
2 tablespoons butter
1 medium onion, finely chopped
1 tablespoon flour
1 teaspoon Dijon mustard
1 teaspoon fresh basil or ½ teaspoon
   dried
1 teaspoon fresh thyme or ½ teaspoon
   dried
1 teaspoon fresh oregano or ½ teaspoon
   dried
1 large clove fresh garlic, minced, or
   ½ teaspoon garlic powder
¼ teaspoon freshly ground black pepper
2 cups milk
8 ounces sharp Cheddar cheese, grated
*Topping*
½ cup butter
1 cup bread crumbs

Cook macaroni until just tender. Do not overcook. Drain and keep warm.

Preheat oven to 400° and grease a 2-quart casserole.

In a heavy, medium saucepan, melt butter and saute onion until transparent. Stir in the flour, mustard, herbs, garlic, and pepper. Stir in the milk and heat, stirring constantly until hot and smooth; do not boil. Remove from heat and stir in three-quarters of the cheese until melted.

Turn macaroni into casserole. Pour on the cheese sauce and stir until well coated. Top with rest of cheese. In a small pan, melt butter and add bread crumbs. Stir until crumbs are coated. Sprinkle crumbs over casserole. Bake, uncovered, for 20 minutes or until bubbly and browned.

Serves 6 to 9 as a side dish or 4 as a main dish.

# *Asparagus Omelet*

*Filling*
1 teaspoon butter
8 stalks fresh asparagus, cut in 1-inch
    pieces
12 to 15 mushrooms, sliced
¼ cup chopped onion
½ teaspoon grated lemon rind
⅛ teaspoon freshly ground black pepper

*Omelet*
4 eggs
2 tablespoons milk
1 teaspoon butter

In a small skillet, melt butter and saute vegetables until tender. Stir in lemon rind and pepper and set aside.

Beat eggs and milk together. Melt butter in a 10-inch skillet. When butter is hot but not browned, pour in eggs. Cook omelet quickly, lifting eggs with spatula to allow uncooked eggs to run underneath. Just before omelet is set, spread filling over half. Fold other half over filling, divide into 2 portions, and remove from skillet.

Serves 2.

The foods Kate and I prepare reflect contentment with our place and our friends. And what flavors wouldn't be enhanced by majestic cabbage palms and fruiting orange trees, by sandhill cranes calling overhead and by moonlight walks around the cypress marsh, by music played on the porch while wood smoke curls out of the chimney. With meals that are soul-warming as well as stomach-pleasing, how can we help but smile smugly when friends gather. We sum it up: Good food, good friends, good times . . . the best recipe we've found.

# Part Two

# Savoring the Seasons

# 5. Spring

The first hints of spring are here, and I am anxious to plant a garden at the Rawlings house. Yellow jessamine is vining through the trees, and the lacy white bloom of wild plums is scattered through the woods. The first fragrance of orange blossoms starts me sorting old seeds and buying new. I press the warm soil firmly over the seeds, patting the earth, leaving fingerprints. My barefoot tracks follow me down the rows. The sun is already hot. Overhead, sandhill cranes are circling, slowly organizing into the purposeful formation that means the end of winter and the beginning of spring. I straighten up my back after planting the seeds and listen as the cranes move on, their familiar call fading northward.

I often imagine growing a garden right up to my kitchen door. I will fill the yard with lush vegetables and flowers and eliminate the fast-growing lawn. Fruit trees will shade the yard, and collard greens will border the steps. I'll walk barefoot through patches of mint and aromatic herbs as they lend their fragrance to the air.

If the nights are warm, the seeds mature quickly. Lettuce, cucumbers, onions, and zucchini squash blend compatibly into satisfying, simple salads complemented by fresh herbs and citrus salad dressings.

## Season's Salad

½ head lettuce
3 tomatoes, cut in wedges
1 cucumber, sliced
4 green onions with tops, sliced
¼ cup chopped fresh basil
¼ cup chopped fresh parsley
½ cup alfalfa sprouts

Shred lettuce into large wooden bowl. Add tomatoes, cucumber, and onions. Sprinkle with herbs and alfalfa sprouts and mix well. Toss with Dessie's Dressing or any favorite.

Serves 4.

Though the city is only 20 miles away, I visit infrequently. The generous yield from gardens, grove, and lakes provides a means of self-sufficiency. I'm not completely independent of the city, however, and when I accumulate enough errands, I head to town.

In the supermarket, I pass shelves of tin cans and cardboard boxes, wishing I could share with other shoppers the fresh fruits and vegetables from the garden. I generally avoid those foods not in season, for they're usually more expensive and less flavorful. My friend Dessie remarked that in her childhood, when something wasn't in season, people just went without it. In my experience, the time spent waiting is well worth it.

## Dessie's Spanish Salad

1 head lettuce
2 tomatoes, sliced
1 cup cooked green beans, cut into
    1-inch pieces
1 cup cooked beets, sliced
6 onion slices (optional)

In 6 individual salad bowls place a layer of torn lettuce, then tomatoes, green beans, and beets. Top with onion slices. Use a mild French dressing made with olive oil.
Serves 6.

## Kohlrabi Sampler

*This is my favorite way to eat kohlrabi fresh from the garden – very simple and very crunchy.*

3 kohlrabi
½ cup lemon juice (approx.)
Salt and pepper to taste

Cut kohlrabi into chunks and place in bowl with lemon juice to cover. Sprinkle with salt and pepper and allow to marinate ½ hour.

# Garden Fresh Slaw

5 cups finely chopped cabbage
2 cups finely chopped lettuce
½ cup chopped fresh parsley
1 cup chopped fresh broccoli heads
2 cups grated carrot
1 cup thinly sliced green onion
1 cup diced onion

*Dressing*
16 ounces plain yogurt
2 tablespoons prepared spicy mustard
⅓ cup salad oil
2 tablespoons wine vinegar
5 medium garlic cloves, crushed
1 teaspoon mixed fines herbs
½ teaspoon celery seed

In a large bowl, combine all the chopped vegetables and mix thoroughly. In a small bowl, combine dressing ingredients in order listed and mix well.

Pour dressing over vegetables and toss. Chill at least 2 hours.
Serves 15.

# Tangy Tarragon Coleslaw

1 medium-sized head of cabbage
½ cup minced fresh parsley

Finely shred cabbage into large mixing bowl. Garnish with parsley. Add Tangy Tarragon Dressing to taste. Refrigerate for 10 minutes.
Serves 6 to 8.

# Tangy Tarragon Dressing

2 cups apple cider vinegar
1½ teaspoons tarragon
1 clove garlic, crushed
1 tablespoon honey
½ teaspoon salt
2 cups salad oil

To vinegar add tarragon, garlic, honey, and salt. Shake well, until honey is dissolved. Allow to steep, preferably 2 to 3 weeks. Then strain and add salad oil.

Mix well before using.

# Early Spring Salad

*This salad is best made from fresh vegetables and herbs picked from a backyard garden in the morning before the sun might wilt the lettuce. The secret to success is using fresh vegetables with flavors that blend compatibly, garden herbs to spice the vegetables, and citrus salad dressings that complement it all.*

1 clove garlic
4 cups lettuce, shredded (preferably
   2 or 3 varieties)
1 cup green onions, sliced
1 cup cucumber, thin-sliced
1 cup yellow squash, thin-sliced
1 cup zucchini squash, grated
3 medium radishes, thin-sliced
1 cup kohlrabi, cut into chunks
¼ cup chopped fresh parsley or
   1 tablespoon dried
¼ cup chopped fresh dill or
   1 tablespoon dried
½ cup snow peas, cut in half

Rub large wooden bowl with one clove of garlic. Shred lettuce loosely and place in bowl. Add sliced onions, including green tops, cucumber, yellow squash, zucchini, radishes, kohlrabi, and herbs and mix. Toss with Sour Orange Sesame Dressing. Garnish with snow peas.

   Serves 4 to 6.

# Spicy Slaw with Peanuts

5 cups cabbage, finely sliced
2 cups turnips, finely grated
1 cup chopped green onions with tops
1 cup peanuts, raw or roasted

Place cabbage, turnips, green onions, and peanuts in bowl and mix well. Add Spicy Garlic Soy Dressing and toss well. Allow to marinate for 15 to 20 minutes before eating, if possible.
Serves 6.

# Grapefruit French Dressing

⅓ cup fresh grapefruit juice
⅓ cup olive oil
⅓ cup salad oil
2 tablespoons cider vinegar
½ teaspoon paprika
¼ teaspoon salt
¼ teaspooon dry mustard
1 clove garlic, crushed (optional)
Honey to taste

Place all ingredients in blender. Mix thoroughly until smooth.
Makes about 1 cup.

# Kate's House Italian Dressing

¼ cup red wine vinegar
2 teaspoons chopped fresh basil or
    1 teaspoon dried
2 teaspoons chopped fresh oregano or
    1 teaspoon dried
1 teaspoon chopped fresh thyme or
    ½ teaspoon dried
1 teaspoon chopped fresh marjoram or
    ½ teaspoon dried
¼ teaspoon grated black pepper
⅓ cup grated Parmesan cheese
¼ cup olive oil
1 cup salad oil

    In a covered jar, mix the vinegar, herbs, and pepper and shake well. Add Parmesan cheese and shake again. Add oils and shake well. Chill.
    Makes 1½ cups.


# Dessie's Herb Wine Vinegar Dressing

⅓ cup oil
⅓ cup apple cider vinegar
⅓ cup dry white wine
½ teaspoon salt
1 teaspoon honey
½ teaspoon oregano
½ teaspoon thyme
½ teaspoon basil

    Mix all ingredients and allow to steep for a month or more. Makes approximately 1 cup.

# Sour Orange Sesame Dressing

2 tablespoons light sesame oil (if not
    available, substitute salad oil)
½ cup salad oil
½ cup sour orange juice (if sweet orange
    juice is substituted, omit honey)
1 tablespoon honey
1 clove garlic, crushed
1 tablespoon sesame seeds
¼ teaspoon salt

Mix all ingredients in blender until creamy. Makes about 1 cup.


# Creamy Yogurt Dressing

1 cup plain yogurt
¼ cup mayonnaise
2 garlic cloves, crushed
2 tablespoons spicy mustard
2 teaspoons chopped fresh basil or
    1 teaspoon dried
2 teaspoons chopped fresh oregano or
    1 teaspoon dried
¼ teaspoon freshly grated black pepper

Combine yogurt and mayonnaise. Stir in other ingredients and beat until light and well blended.

Makes 1¼ cups.

# Lemon Poppy Seed Dressing

1 tablespoon poppy seeds
¼ cup olive oil
½ cup salad oil
⅓ cup honey
1 clove garlic, pressed
¼ teaspoon dry mustard
1 teaspoon finely grated lemon peel
½ cup lemon juice

Place poppy seeds, oil, and honey in blender and blend until well-mixed. Add garlic, mustard, lemon peel, and lemon juice and blend until creamy.

Makes approximately 1½ cups.


# Lemon Bleu-Cheese Dressing

½ cup crumbled bleu cheese
1 clove crushed garlic
¼ cup lemon juice
½ cup lowfat yogurt
¼ teaspoon black pepper
½ teaspoon soy sauce

Crumble bleu cheese into medium bowl. Add garlic and lemon juice and mash with a fork, leaving some chunks of cheese. Add yogurt, pepper, and soy sauce and mix well. Adjust seasonings to taste.

Makes about 1 cup.

Note: This also makes a good vegetable dip.

# Spicy Garlic Soy Dressing

½ cup oil
½ cup vinegar
1 teaspoon honey
1 tablespoon soy sauce
1 clove garlic, pressed
1 teaspoon jalapeno pepper, minced
   (or 1 teaspoon datil pepper sauce)
Black pepper to taste

   Mix together oil, vinegar, honey, and soy sauce. Add garlic, jalepeno pepper, and black pepper and shake well before pouring over slaw.
   Makes approximately 1 cup.


# Japanese Dressing

½ cup miso (Japanese bean paste)
¼ cup water
¼ cup rice vinegar or white vinegar
½ cup salad oil
2 teaspoons grated fresh ginger
1 teaspoon grated lemon rind

   Mix miso and water to a smooth paste. Add remaining ingredients and beat with a whisk until well blended.
   Makes 1½ cups.

# Cross Creek Tea Blend

*If these ingredients don't grow in your garden, buy them at local markets or health food stores.*

3 cups dried mint leaves, finely chopped
1 cup dried lemongrass, finely chopped
¼ cup jasmine flower tea
¼ cup dried orange peel, finely chopped

Mix mint, lemongrass, jasmine flower tea, and orange peel in a large glass jar. Keep tightly sealed. Fill half-pint jars with mixture for gifts or fill small cloth bags for fragrant sachets.


# Citrus Vinegar

1 cup apple cider vinegar
½ cup orange juice

Mix vinegar and orange juice together in Mason jar and allow to steep several weeks. Add a garlic clove and fresh herbs, such as basil, oregano, or dill, if desired. Use for flavoring salad dressings or in any recipe to replace regular vinegar.

Makes about 1½ cups.


*Impromptu Music Suppers*

Many of our friends live in the communities of Micanopy, McIntosh, Cross Creek, and Grove Park, which are among the oldest towns in Florida. Here, the cracker style houses, set among stands of pine and live oak, retain the character of old Florida. We are attracted to this area because we find satisfaction in blending things of value from the past into the present. As in Marjorie Rawlings' day, some of us live off the land as farmers and fishermen. Others are craftsmen and artisans, beekeepers, horse trainers, and retirees. There are also shopkeepers, librarians, professors, and technicians who commute to nearby cities.

Though most of the folks aren't more than a fifteen minute drive from each other, we go for quite a while without visiting. When we do get together, we prefer informal and spontaneous gatherings out-of-doors, with the focus on good food and lively music. When guitars, fiddles, and banjos tune up, we become so absorbed in the music that we forget about eating, but not for long. Everyone contributes to the meal, and we are constantly amazed by the compatibility of the foods. After dinner, the music begins again and lasts far into the night.

# Miso Vegetable Soup

1 tablespoon cooking oil
1 medium onion, chopped
1 medium carrot, chopped
1 medium zucchini or yellow squash,
    chopped
6 cups chicken stock
2 cups chopped spinach or cabbage
¼ cup Japanese bean paste (miso)
1 cake tofu (8 oz.), cut in cubes

In a large pot, heat oil. Add onion, carrot, and squash and saute 2 minutes. Add chicken stock, bring to boil and simmer, covered, until vegetables are tender, about 5 minutes. Add spinach or cabbage and cook 1 minute.

Remove ¼ cup of hot stock from pot and mix with bean paste until smooth. Return mixture to pot, turn off heat, and stir through. Add tofu and stir.

Serves 6.

# Indian Corn Soup

1 tablespoon oil
1 cup green spring onions, sliced
1 cup diced turnips
1 cup fresh corn, removed from cob
1½ quarts chicken broth
Salt and pepper

Heat oil in 2-quart saucepan. Reserve ¼ cup green onion tops for garnish. Saute remaining onions until soft. Add turnips and cook 5 minutes. Cut whole corn kernels from cob. Stir into onion mixture, and cook 5 minutes longer.

Add chicken broth and simmer briefly until vegetables are tender. Add salt and pepper to taste. Garnish with sliced green onion tops.

Serves 4 to 6.

# Taco the Town

1 3-pound baking chicken
1 large avocado
½ pound sharp white Cheddar cheese
Taco sauce (see recipe)
8 to 12 corn tortillas

Bake whole chicken in 350° oven until done. Allow to cool, then remove skin and slice in long, thin pieces. Cut avocado in half and scoop out pulp. Cut into small chunks. Grate cheese. Heat tortillas.

Put chicken, avocado, cheese, and tortillas on separate serving plates and let guests help themselves, adding taco sauce to taste.

Serves 4 to 6.

# Sticky Steve's Oyster Pie (actually an omelet)

1 tablespoon butter
2 cloves garlic, pressed
4 dozen raw oysters, washed and
     drained
½ teaspoon hot sauce (optional)
1 onion, cut in ⅛-inch thick rounds
1 green pepper, cut in ⅛-inch thick
     rounds
2 tomatoes, cut in ¼-inch thick rounds
¼ teaspoon oregano
¼ teaspoon black pepper
1 cup small whole mushrooms
10 eggs, separated
¼ cup milk
Paprika

Heat butter in Dutch oven or 10-inch cast iron skillet. Add garlic, then oysters. Sprinkle with hot sauce and stir. Simmer oysters until you've eaten 1 dozen (or 10 minutes).

Preheat oven to 350°. Layer onion, green pepper, and tomatoes over oysters, making 2 layers of each. Sprinkle with oregano and black pepper. Add mushrooms. Cover and let steam in oyster liquid for 5 minutes.

Beat egg whites and yolks separately. Stir together adding milk. Pour eggs into skillet, sprinkle with paprika, and bake uncovered for 20 minutes. Remove from oven and serve immediately.

Serves 6.

# Cashew Chicken and Vegetables

2 boneless chicken breasts, cut into
    bite-sized pieces
2 tablespoons cooking oil
1 cup raw unsalted cashews
1 large sweet onion, halved and sliced
1 medium carrot, sliced
1 medium zucchini, cut into chunks
2 yellow squash, cut in chunks
1 cup sliced mushrooms
1 cup fresh spinach or cabbage,
    coarsely chopped
1 tablespoon chopped fresh ginger
1 garlic clove, minced or crushed
¼ cup soy sauce
¾ cup water
2 tablespoons corn starch

In a large skillet or wok, heat oil over high heat for 30 seconds. Add cashews and stir fry until browned, stirring constantly, about 2 minutes. Remove pan from heat. Remove cashews from oil and set aside.

Return pan to medium high heat. Add onion and carrot; stir fry 3 minutes. Add zucchini and yellow squash; stir fry 3 minutes. Add chicken pieces; stir fry 2 minutes. Add mushrooms and spinach or cabbage; stir fry 2 minutes. Add ginger and garlic; stir fry 1 minute. Push ingredients to one side of pan.

Quickly mix cornstarch with water and soy sauce. Pour into pan, stir until it thickens and clears, and mix all ingredients into sauce. Stir in cashews.

Serve hot over brown rice.

Serves 4.

# It's Salad Time

*When my sister Mary says, "It's salad time," we look forward to her specialty. It's a meal in itself or may be served with bread and soup.*

8 small red potatoes
¾ cup apple cider vinegar
½ cup salad oil
1 clove garlic
2 overflowing cups lettuce, cut in
    fine strips
1 overflowing cup spinach, cut in
    fine strips
1 cup sprouts, preferably alfalfa and
    mung bean sprouts mixed
1 medium onion, diced
2 medium carrots, diced
½ cup celery, diced
½ cup fresh mushrooms, sliced
2 tablespoons lemon juice
3 hard-boiled eggs, thinly sliced
2 medium tomatoes, cut in wedges
½ cup sunflower seeds
¼ cup fresh parsley (or 1 Tbsp. dried)
¼ cup fresh dill (or 1 Tbsp. dried)
½ cup cottage cheese or tofu (optional)
½ cup black olives (optional)

Cut unpeeled potatoes into quarters and boil until just tender. Marinate overnight in mixture of oil and vinegar.

Crush garlic and rub the salad bowl with it. Combine lettuce, spinach, and sprouts in the bowl with onion, carrots, celery and mushrooms. Add lemon juice and toss. Add eggs, tomatoes, and sunflower seeds. Use scissors to snip fresh parsley and dill into small pieces. Mix herbs, cottage cheese (or tofu) and olives with other ingredients.

Drain the potatoes and add them to the salad. The secret of this salad is in the variety of textures of the ingredients.

Add dressing and toss the salad well. Tangy Tarragon Dressing is Mary's personal favorite. We also recommend Creamy Yogurt Dressing.

Serves 4 to 6.

# Chicken and New Potato Salad

15 to 18 small new potatoes, unpeeled,
    cut into bite-sized chunks
2 cups cooked chicken, cut into small
    pieces
½ cup chopped green onion
1 cup fresh broccoli or spinach, finely
    chopped
1 cup grated carrot
*Dressing*
1 cup plain yogurt
2 tablespoons mayonnaise
1 teaspoon prepared mustard
2 medium cloves garlic, crushed
1 teaspoon fresh, finely chopped basil
    or ½ teaspoon dried
1 teaspoon fresh, finely chopped
    oregano or ½ teaspoon dried
¼ teaspoon freshly ground black pepper

Cook potatoes until just tender. In a large bowl, combine chicken, potatoes, and vegetables and mix well. In a small bowl, combine dressing ingredients and blend well.

Pour dressing over salad and toss. Chill at least 2 hours.

Serves 8.

# Tarragon Mushroom Omelet

*Filling*

1 teaspoon butter
1 small onion, chopped
12 to 15 mushrooms, sliced
½ cup chopped fresh parsley
1 teaspoon tarragon
¼ teaspoon black pepper
½ cup bread crumbs
1 egg, beaten

*Omelet*

1 teaspoon butter
4 eggs
2 tablespoons milk

In a small skillet, melt butter and saute onion until transparent. Add mushrooms and cook until tender. Add parsley, tarragon, and pepper and cook until parsley is limp. Stir in bread crumbs. Add 1 beaten egg and cook, stirring, until set. Remove from heat and set aside.

Beat 4 eggs with milk. Melt butter in a 10-inch skillet. When butter is hot but not browned, pour in eggs. Cook omelet quickly, lifting edges with spatula to allow uncooked egg to run underneath. Just before omelet is set, spread filling over half. Fold other half over filling, divide into 2 portions, and remove immediately from skillet.

Serves 2.

# Mom's Cheese Souffle

4 tablespoons butter or margarine
6 tablespoons flour
1 cup milk
1 teaspoon salt (or to taste)
½ cup grated Cheddar cheese
6 eggs, separated

Preheat oven to 350°. Melt butter; stir in flour slowly. Warm the milk and add gradually, stirring constantly until the mixture is smooth. Stir in salt and cheese. Remove from heat. Cool.

Beat egg yolks until lemon colored, then stir in cooled cheese mixture. Beat egg whites until stiff and fold into mixture. Bake in greased 9-inch round casserole dish for 30 minutes.

## Cornbread

Cornbread belongs in a category all its own. It's a staple in our kitchens today as it has been in the South for generations. Easy to make, it's the natural accompaniment for cooked greens as well as for salads, soups, and fish.

Kate and I used to think that everyone liked cornbread until our friend Charlie confessed that he had hated it from childhood. He told us this with a mixture of fear and relief — fear that he might not be invited to dinner again and relief that he wouldn't have to force down any more cornbread. Our friendship survived these differences, of course, and Kate and I continue to serve cornbread regularly, although not to Charlie. We enjoy varying the ingredients to create many delicious versions of this versatile southern specialty.

# Our Staple Cornbread

1½ cups cornmeal
½ cup whole wheat flour
1 teaspoon baking powder
½ teaspoon baking soda
½ teaspoon salt
1½ cups buttermilk
   or 1 cup yogurt and ½ cup milk
2 eggs, beaten
1 tablespoon butter

Preheat oven to 375°. Stir together cornmeal, whole wheat flour, baking powder, baking soda, and salt. Blend yogurt, milk, and egg. Add liquid to dry ingredients, stirring just until ingredients are blended thoroughly.

Butter a 9½-inch (#7) cast-iron skillet (or 8 x 8 pan), and heat in oven until sizzling. Remove skillet from oven, tilting to coat bottom and sides evenly. Pour batter into hot skillet. Bake at 375° for ½ hour or until done.

Makes approximately 8 servings.

# Cornbread Variations

### Pecan Cornbread

Add ½ cup chopped pecans to basic batter.

### Molasses Cornbread

Add 3 tablespoons molasses to liquids in basic batter. Or cane syrup may be used.

### Sesame Cornbread

Pour basic cornbread batter into baking pan, sprinkle with 3 table-spoons sesame seeds, and bake.

### Crunchy Cornbread

Add 1 cup fresh corn, cut off the cob to basic batter. Or you can substitute an 8-ounce can, drained.

### Mexican Cornbread

To the Crunchy Cornbread recipe, add 2 tablespoons minced jalapeno peppers and ½ cup grated sharp Cheddar cheese. Pour into greased, heated 9½-inch cast-iron skillet. Sprinkle with an additional ½ cup Cheddar cheese.

### Creole Cornbread

Add 1 teaspoon "shrimp boil herbs" to the basic batter.

# Holiday Cornbread

1 cup whole wheat flour
1 teaspoon baking powder
1 teaspoon baking soda
1 teaspoon nutmeg
1 cup white or yellow cornmeal
1 egg, beaten
2 medium bananas, mashed
½ cup plain yogurt
1 cup prepared eggnog
3 tablespoons molasses (unsulfured)

Preheat oven to 375°. Sift together flour, baking powder, baking soda, and nutmeg. Stir in the cornmeal. In a smaller bowl, combine remaining ingredients and blend well. Add wet ingredients to dry and stir until well blended.

Pour into a greased 8 x 8 baking dish and bake at 375° for 25 to 30 minutes.


# Post-Holiday Cornbread

1 cup unprocessed bran
½ cup boiling water
2 cups whole wheat flour
2 teaspoons baking powder
1 teaspoon baking soda
1 cup cornmeal
2 eggs, beaten
1½ cups milk
½ cup unsulfured molasses
3 tablespoons honey

Preheat oven to 375°. Mix bran with boiling water and allow to stand 20 minutes. In a medium bowl, sift together flour, baking powder, and baking soda. Stir in cornmeal. Combine the eggs, milk, molasses, and honey and mix well; add to dry ingredients and stir only until blended.

Pour into a greased 9 x 14 baking pan and bake at 375° for 30 minutes.

# Banana Cornbread

1 cup cornmeal
1 cup whole wheat flour
2 teaspoons baking powder
1 teaspoon nutmeg
2 ripe bananas, mashed
    with a fork
1 egg, beaten
½ cup milk
½ cup plain yogurt

Preheat oven to 375°. In a medium bowl, combine cornmeal, flour, baking powder and nutmeg. In a small bowl, mix mashed bananas, egg, milk, and yogurt and beat with a whisk until well blended. Add wet ingredients to dry and mix only until all ingredients are moistened.

Pour into a greased 8 x 8 x 2 baking pan. Bake at 375° for 25 to 30 minutes or until knife inserted in center comes out clean.

Early one morning while the spring air was still cool, I made breakfast on the woodstove in Marjorie's kitchen. My brother "Sticky" Steve was visiting, so I invited him and a few friends for music and muffins. I waited by the stove for the first pleasant crackling and warmth of the wood fire, then went to the chicken coop for fresh eggs. As wood smoke curled out the chimney, I picked tender small zucchini and spring herbs from the garden. My neighbor Tom played "Blackberry Blossom" on the guitar while Steve's fiddle picked up the melody. I put my special baked zucchini omelettes and some muffins into the oven and joined in on the banjo. Betty found a set of spoons in the kitchen drawer and carried the rhythm; others kept time with their feet. Music filled the yard while the savory scent of orange bran muffins and freshly ground coffee drifted through the house.

# Baked Zucchini Omelet

1 tablespoon butter
½ cup spring green onions
½ cup mixed fresh herbs: dill, parsley, tarragon
1 cup finely grated zucchini
8 eggs
¼ cup yogurt (milk or water may be substituted)
¼ teaspoon black pepper

Preheat oven to 300°. In a 10-inch skillet, brown onions in butter. Add herbs and zucchini, stirring together. Remove from heat.

Beat eggs with yogurt, pepper, and salt until light. Pour over zucchini mixture and bake until set, about 15 minutes.

Serves 4.

# Banana Orange Bran Muffins

1 cup orange juice
3 cups unprocessed bran
2 teaspoons grated orange rind
2 eggs
3 ripe bananas, mashed
½ cup orange blossom honey
1 cup plain yogurt
2 cups whole wheat flour
½ cup soy flour or corn meal
2½ teaspoons baking soda

Preheat oven to 375°. Heat orange juice until simmering. In a large bowl, mix orange juice, bran, and orange rind and let stand. In a medium bowl, beat eggs. Add mashed banana, honey, and yogurt and beat well. Mix with bran.

Sift together the flours and soda and fold into bran mixture. Pour into greased muffin tins. Bake at 375° for 20 minutes.

Makes 2 dozen muffins.

*Gingerbread Waffle Auction*

Our all-time favorite get-together at the Creek was the "Gingerbread Waffle Auction." Now remembered wistfully by those fortunate enough to have attended, it was one of those spontaneous occasions that can never be re-created.

Kate and I both had a houseful of visiting family and friends, and someone suggested a breakfast party at my house. The day couldn't have been a finer one for welcoming spring. It was mid-February, and the sky was clear blue and cloudless. A few oranges still hung on the trees, and the red-birds were building their nests. When I commented that it was too fine a day to be stuck in the kitchen, a few of the "long hungrys" decided that it was their turn to cook. With some misgivings, I relinquished my kitchen to them.

My brother Steve found an assortment of aprons for the four ambitious cooks. Nick was in charge of the gingerbread waffles, and mixed three large bowls of batter to be sure there would be enough. Tom busied himself at the stove making his maple syrup custard topping while his brother Don set up long plank tables under the orange trees. Stretching extension cords through the windows, they had four waffle irons steaming at once. Whether deftly pouring batter from large ladles or opening the waffle irons at exactly the right moment to reveal the crisp waffles, the cooks enjoyed the full attention of twenty hungry onlookers.

# Gingerbread Waffles

1½ cups whole wheat flour
1½ cups unbleached white flour
2 teaspoons ginger
½ teaspoon each nutmeg, cinnamon,
    and cloves
2 teaspoons baking powder
2 teaspoons baking soda
6 eggs, lightly beaten
2 cups yogurt or buttermilk
½ cup oil
1 cup cane syrup or molasses

Start the waffle iron smoking. Sift together dry ingredients. Beat eggs lightly, blend in yogurt. Mix together oil and cane syrup and blend well with eggs and yogurt. Stir dry ingredients into liquid, mixing quickly and thoroughly, but do not stir any more than necessary.

Use a pitcher or ladle for pouring the batter into heated waffle iron. Makes about fourteen 5 x 5-inch waffles.

Pecan waffles and crispy corn waffles browned to perfection as the spicy smell of gingerbread waffles floated on the air. From my pantry we took fresh orange syrup, roselle syrup, pear butter, tangerine butter spread, and Steve's honey. Kate brought over her stock of blueberry-lemon jam, kumquat butter, and maple syrup. Unfortunately, the maple syrup custard topping that Tom had so meticulously concocted was poured into a waffle iron. But the messy mistake was soon forgotten when Steve hollered, "Don't starve folks! Let's eat!" The guests hesitated at the serving table, unable to choose from the delicious assortment. However, when the cooks pretended to "auction" their culinary creations, the bidding was fast-paced.

# Crispy Corn Waffles

2 eggs, beaten
1¾ cups milk
1 cup whole wheat flour
1 cup cornmeal
2 teaspoons baking powder
4 tablespoons light cooking oil plus
    more for oiling waffle iron

Combine ingredients in order listed, and mix with a few quick strokes. Do not beat.

Heat waffle iron until very hot. Brush with cooking oil and fill ⅔ full. Close lid and cook until steam stops escaping from sides.

Makes 6 waffles.

# Orange Honey Syrup

*I usually make a small amount at a time and keep a jar or two refrigerated, ready for the next batch of waffles or pancakes.*

1½ cups orange juice
½ cup lemon juice
½ cup honey (preferably orange
 blossom)
2 tablespoons orange peel, finely grated

Heat orange and lemon juice in 3-quart enamel or stainless steel saucepan. Add honey and orange peel, stirring until honey is dissolved. Bring to a boil and simmer for 10 minutes, stirring frequently.
 Makes about 1½ cups.

# Virginia's Orange Butter

½ pound butter, softened
½ pound margarine, softened
½ cup sweet, tasty orange juice
 (tangerine, temple orange, or
 tangelo especially recommended)
2 tablespoons orange rind, finely
 grated.

Whip butter and margarine with electric mixer for at least 6 minutes. Then whip in orange juice, 1 tablespoon at a time. Blend in well after each addition. Blend in orange rind by hand.
 This is very flavorful served on biscuits, rolls, toast, or waffles. Also good on hot baked sweet potatoes and other vegetables.

# Blueberry Lemon Jam

12 cups fresh blueberries
1 large lemon
1 teaspoon nutmeg
2 cups sugar

In a large pot, crush 2 cups blueberries. Slice lemon into paper-thin slices. Add to crushed blueberries and bring to slow boil. Add remaining blueberries and cook, stirring, until almost tender. Add sugar and nutmeg. Stir and cook over low heat until a small amount dropped on a plate will stay in place, about 30 minutes. Follow standard canning process for storage or make small batch for immediate use. (Important: contact your county extension office home economist or consult USDA bulletin #56 for complete and safe canning instructions.)

Makes about 4 pints.

# Kumquat Butter

4 pounds kumquats
2 cups water
3 cups sugar or 2 cups honey

Wash kumquats well and remove any blemishes with a sharp knife. Cut in half and squeeze out the seeds. Chop fruit coarsely with a food chopper using a medium blade.

In a 4-quart enamel pot, combine chopped fruit and water and bring to a slow boil. Simmer, covered, for 20 minutes, stirring frequently. Remove from heat and allow to sit 8 to 10 hours to develop pectin. The next day bring fruit mixture to boil, add sugar or honey, and simmer slowly, uncovered, for about 30 minutes or until the kumquat peel is translucent and the mixture has the consistency of apple butter. Follow standard canning process for storage or make a small batch for immediate use. (Important: contact your county extension office home economist or consult USDA bulletin #56 for complete and safe canning instructions.)

Makes 4 to 5 pints.

The gingerbread waffles, new to most of us, were everyone's favorite. After the last of the batter was gone, we relaxed in lawn chairs in the warm sun. The silence was broken now and then by the hum of a bee in search of new orange blossoms or by the thud of the last of winter's oranges dropping to the ground.

*Rooster and Rice*

The chickens I brought from home prospered at the Rawlings house and began to lay good brown eggs. Perched on the rusty sickle mower or chasing bugs about the yard, the fowl foursome added new life to the place.

During my first few months on the job, while still living at the Rawlings place, I had to attend Ranger Academy near Orlando for the two weeks of intensive training required of all Florida park rangers. It was then that the troubles started. While I was away studying resource management and learning to pour cement and to identify the sweet gum tree, some low-living dog got bored one Sunday and trotted over to dig under the chicken pen. It was the preacher's dog, no less! He feasted on all four chickens plus the two mallard drakes. I related the incident to an old-timer friend at the Creek and he listened thoughtfully to my lament. "You know, Hon," he responded, "it's a fact that preachers like chicken, and I reckon it follows their dogs would, too."

A man from Island Grove offered me a game hen and rooster to get started again. I drove over to pick them up, but discovered I'd forgotten a box to put them in. Undaunted, the man deftly tied the hen's legs together and put her in a paper bag. He followed suit with the rooster, who immediately tore through the bag with his spurs. Then I remembered a large canning kettle I had in the truck and as we lowered the hapless rooster in, the man quipped, "Now, there's you a chicken in the pot. All you need is boiling water." Muffled metallic squawks accompanied me the three miles back to Cross Creek.

That spring the mother hen hatched a large brood and roamed the yard with a trail of small biddies. Though most folks contend that chickens are downright dumb, game chickens have an innate resourcefulness when allowed to roam freely. They are wary of wild predators and more adaptable than many domestic varieties. This was the same hardy breed that Marjorie had inherited with the place, and I became fond of them, considering myself a foster mother of sorts.

Confident that everything was secure, I took a short vacation, leaving my co-worker, Bob, a reminder. "Please water the chickens." I returned a few days later to his candid note, "What chickens? . . . as of Saturday night." Something had dug under the pen and left nothing but chicken feathers. I began to wonder if we were meant to raise chickens at all.

It wasn't long, though, before I began waking to blood-curdling squawks that would leave me wide-awake before dawn. A silence would follow, leaving no doubt that a "varmint" had gotten what it was after. Sure enough, one less chicken would appear for corn in the morning. Besides the local dogs, many raccoons, foxes, and possums still lurked in the woods. As the pillaging continued, I became alarmed. A few chickens could be spared now and then, but we were down to one black hen, one yellow one, and two roosters. We strengthened the pen with new wire and all went well for some weeks.

To replenish our stock, Kingsley Plantation, another state historic site nearby, sent us some of their surplus game chickens, a mama hen and nine one-week-old biddies. As the biddies

matured, we found we had too many roosters, so we let three extras free to fend for themselves. I feared they might fight, but instead they became inseparable. We called them the "three stooges." In the mornings they would run headlong, single file, from the grove or woods for their scratch feed. If one chased a bug, the others followed in hot pursuit. In late afternoon as the sun's rays slanted through the grove, the roosters' jaunty combs were illumined a transparent red. Their iridescent tail feathers curled and bobbed above the tall grass as they strutted about their business. When they even began to crow in unison, a disgruntled neighbor commented, "How many chickens do you have *now?*"

They took to roosting in the magnolia tree close to my bedroom window. Not only did they start crowing before dawn, they persisted for several hours. Many mornings, in a vain attempt to calm myself back to sleep, I would count the seconds in each interval of silence; the tranquility would last about 16 seconds. Usually this worked, but that morning I just couldn't relax since I had overnight guests, who certainly did not expect the predawn rooster reveille. I hoped their night's sleep could be prolonged, but the crowing continued. I stormed from my bed. Standing under the tree, I chucked a few magnolia pods at the offending roosters and startled them off their roosts. With a few parting shrieks, they fled to the woods. I think that was when I decided to make roosters a part of my cooking demonstrations.

Now we manage to raise enough chickens each year to keep ahead of the varmints' voracity and to set the table, too. Since one rooster is plenty in the yard, I cook the surplus roosters while they're still young and tender. I've substituted rooster for chicken in some of Marjorie's dishes that I prepare to demonstrate the woodstove to visitors. Her chicken and yellow rice becomes rooster and rice, which not only feeds the employees at the Rawlings place, but satisfies my quiet-loving neighbors at the same time.

## Spring Greens and Spring Chicken

*Old-timers considered early spring greens to be a blood cleanser or purifier. After the winter, when the garden greens had frozen, they would pick wild poke, dandelion, or mustard greens to make a restorative, invigorating "tonic."*

*With the first burst of spring growth, when the turnip greens, mustard greens, or collards from the garden are especially tender, I simmer them slowly with a whole chicken (or rooster, depending on the surplus). Substituting chicken for the traditional ham hock results in a flavorful broth that can be further enhanced by the addition of a hot pepper or two.*

1 tablespoon butter
½ cup chopped green onions, with tops
1 clove garlic, minced
1 spring chicken, hopefully 2 pounds
    and tender, cut in individual pieces
2 or 3 hot peppers (optional)
1 "mess" of tender spring greens
    (a mixture of turnip, mustard and
    collard greens — enough chopped
    greens to loosely fill a 3-quart pan.
    They will cook down.)
Salt and pepper, to taste

In a 3-quart cook-pot, saute onion and garlic in butter. Brown chicken quickly on both sides. Add hot peppers and water to cover. Cover with lid and simmer until tender. Remove the chicken; allow to cool. Bring the chicken broth to a boil and add half the greens. Turn heat to low and cook, covered, until greens cook down (5 minutes or so). Add the rest of the greens and simmer uncovered only until the greens are tender. Don't overcook.

Remove chicken from bones and cut in bite-size pieces. Serve in individual bowls with the tender greens and some of the broth. A little hot pepper vinegar and a pan of cornbread round out the meal.

Serves 4 to 6.

*Canoe Picnics*

We celebrate spring from February right into summer with canoe trips, horseback rides, and picnics. At the first suggestion of an outing, Kate and I reach for our picnic baskets. In no time we have a menu in mind. We put canoes in Cross Creek and drift the half-mile downstream into Orange Lake. Once there, we watch the ospreys diving for fish and sample Kate's latest batch of Southern pecan granola. Sometimes we just have blueberry muffins with cinnamon coffee. We are soothed by the water lapping at the sides of the canoe, the birds calling overhead, the expanses of water and sky.

# Southern Pecan Granola

12 cups rolled oats
1 cup unprocessed bran
3 cups chopped pecans
2 cups unsweetened coconut flakes
1 cup light oil
1 cup cane syrup or light molasses
½ cup honey
1 tablespoon vanilla

Preheat oven to 400°. In a very large bowl, mix oats, bran, pecans, and coconut. In a saucepan, mix oil, cane syrup, and honey and heat until warm and well blended. Do not boil. Stir in vanilla.

Pour liquid ingredients over dry and mix thoroughly. Spread mixture ½ inch thick on greased cookie sheets.

Bake 10 minutes, turn in sections and bake 5 minutes longer. Cool on waxed paper. Store in glass jars.

Makes about 18 cups.

If we paddle steadily upstream on Cross Creek, it doesn't take long to reach Lake Lochloosa. We've left our watches behind on purpose, and as the canoe glides quietly among cypress trees we lose all sense of time. We float under the high cypress canopy, watching an eagle catch his breakfast and carry it back to his tree. An alligator, showing just his snout and a few fluted lines of his back, watches us warily and then swims away, his powerful tail rippling the surface.

When the sun is high and hot, we guess at the hour — "It's about noon-30" — and eagerly unload the picnic baskets.

For the longer trip to Alexander Springs, a group of us pack the cars the night before and leave as the sun rises. In a few hours we're floating over the springs, watching the morning mist coil around the canoes, and staring into the aquamarine depths of the bubbling spring. We paddle on into the river, passing small islands and palm-studded woods. Turtles sun-bake on logs, and fish dart through the perfectly clear water. When we're halfway along on our trip, the water becomes dark and rich-hued, and as the river widens, it flows through long grassy stretches. We tie the canoe to a fallen pine tree and can hardly wait to get Jack's Florida chicken and Kate's lemon parsley potato salad out of the picnic basket. There's coffee for those whose eyes might not yet be open wide to the wonders all around and cold ale or tall thermoses of iced mint tea for the rest of us.

# Jack's Florida Chicken

1 3-pound frying chicken, cut into
    serving pieces
2 cloves garlic, cut into halves
½ cup lime or lemon juice
⅓ cup soy sauce
3 tablespoons cooking oil
2 medium onions, diced
Salt to taste (preferably herbal salt)

Wash chicken and rub with garlic. Marinate overnight in refrigerator in a mixture of lime juice, soy sauce, and garlic. Turn occasionally.

Heat oil in deep frying pan. Add chicken, sprinkle with salt, and brown over high heat. Reduce heat and add onions and marinade. Cover and simmer 45 minutes to 1 hour.

Serves 4.

Variation: Jack's real specialty is barbecuing outside over a grill, for which he recommends cooking the marinated chicken in foil, bone side down, for 30 minutes, then 10 minutes on the other side, brushing frequently with marinade.

# Braided Onion Bread

4½ cups unbleached white flour
2 cups whole wheat flour
½ cup corn meal
1 package dry yeast
¼ cup warm water
¾ cup plain yogurt
¼ cup milk
1 envelope onion soup mix
¼ teaspoon baking soda
2 tablespoons sugar
3 tablespoons melted butter
3 eggs
1 cup warm water
½ cup chopped onion
3 cloves garlic, crushed
1 teaspoon sweet basil
½ cup sesame seeds

Sift flours together in a medium bowl. Add yeast to ¼ cup water; stir and set aside. In a large bowl, combine yogurt, milk, soup mix, baking soda, sugar, butter, 2 beaten eggs, and 1 cup water. Stir in onion, garlic, basil, and yeast.

Add flour gradually while mixing, until a stiff dough is formed. Turn out onto floured board and knead until smooth and elastic, about 10 minutes. Place dough in a large oiled pan; turn so top is greased. Cover with a towel and let rise in a warm place until doubled in bulk, about 1½ to 2 hours.

Punch dough down. Divide in half. Cut each half into thirds. Roll each piece into a long strip about 1 inch thick. Pinch 3 strips together at one end and braid loosely, pinching the ends together. Place loaves on greased cookie sheet, brush with oil, cover, and let rise 45 minutes.

Brush loaves with 1 egg, beaten, and sprinkle with sesame seeds. Bake at 350° for 40 minutes to an hour or until they sound hollow when thumped.   Makes 2 loaves.

# Lemon Parsley Potato Salad

15 medium new potatoes, unpeeled
1 small onion, chopped
½ cup chopped fresh parsley
1 teaspoon chopped fresh marjoram or
    ½ teaspoon dried
1 teaspoon chopped fresh thyme or
    ½ teaspoon dried
2 tablespoons grated lemon rind
¼ cup lemon juice
¾ cup plain unsweetened yogurt

Wash potatoes and cut into quarters. Steam or boil until tender. Drain. Blend all other ingredients and mix with potatoes while still hot. Chill at least 3 hours.
    Serves 6.

# Mildred's Tea Cakes

3 to 4 cups unbleached white flour
1 cup whole wheat pastry flour
2 teaspoons baking powder
¼ pound butter
2 teaspoons cooking oil
1 teaspoon vanilla
1½ cups cane syrup
4 eggs, beaten

Preheat oven to 350°. Sift together 3 cups of white flour with whole wheat flour and baking powder.

Melt butter and add cooking oil and vanilla. Put in medium bowl and combine with cane syrup and beaten eggs. Stir liquid ingredients into flour mixture. Mix well, adding remaining flour until the dough is no longer sticky. Place on floured board and knead briefly. Roll the dough out ½-inch thick and cut into 3 inch rounds.

Place on greased baking sheet and brown real well at 350°.

Makes 2 to 3 dozen large "cakes" or cookies that disappear quickly!

### Lochloosa Marsh Rides

For a day's horseback ride to Lochloosa marsh, we fill the saddle bags with a light picnic. Following the tantalizing call of sandhill cranes to the marsh's edge, we ride over open sand trails and through pine woods and palmettos. We spread our jackets on the warm dusty ground and enjoy our trailside meal of sharp Cheddar cheese and rings of dried figs, with energy muffins, cold baked sweet potatoes, and thirst-quenching apples and oranges.

# Hi-Energy Muffins

4 cups whole wheat flour

2 cups wheat germ

1 teaspoon baking powder

1 teaspoon baking soda

1 teaspoon cinnamon

1 teaspoon nutmeg

½ teaspoon ginger

½ teaspoon allspice

1 cup raisins

1 cup chopped dried apricots

1 cup chopped dried figs

1 cup chopped walnuts or pecans

1 cup chopped peeled apple

2 eggs, beaten

2 cups milk

½ cup cane syrup or honey

¼ cup dark molasses

Preheat oven to 375°. Into a large bowl, sift flour, baking powder, baking soda, and spices. Stir in wheat germ, chopped fruits, and nuts. In a small bowl, mix the eggs, milk, cane syrup or honey, and molasses. Pour wet ingredients into dry and stir just until all ingredients have been moistened.

Fill greased muffin tins two-thirds full. Bake at 375° for 20 minutes or until golden brown.

Makes 2 dozen muffins.

# 6. Summer

Summer in Florida lasts much longer than the three months allotted to it on the calendar. It overlaps both spring and fall with long hot days and humid nights. The heat reduces our sense of urgency about getting things done and allows us a welcome rest. Even the busiest among us learns to slow down. Some friends leave for the Carolina mountains or the beach. Those of us who stay settle in with the heat. We sweat and complain, but we adjust and find camaraderie in accepting summer for what it is.

A friend writes from Wyoming, and I hear her longing for the Florida she grew up in:

*I hear the Spanish moss whispering against rusty screens*
*while you sit on the porch reading with a tiny light*
*trying not to attract any more mosquitoes than necessary.*
*Sweaty fingerprints on the page, a few drops of pina colada …*

The Rawlings house is well-suited to Florida's hot climate. Designed with ample windows, doors, and breezeways for cross-ventilation, the house is naturally air-conditioned. Porches shade the interior and high ceilings hold the cool air overnight. I sit on the porch sheltered from the hot sun or just out of reach of a downpour, relishing the cool droplets of rain after a sticky summer day. I can feel the rain misting through the screens, watch the trees soaking up the moisture and the citrus leaves glistening. The ducks chortle, and the chickens chase after bugs in the wet grass.

There is rarely a hot summer day without a breeze stirring across the porches and through the breezeways. Those few days without a breeze are long and memorable. I recall one such day when the temperature soared to 102°. The sky was bleached and the air perfectly still. When dusk fell, the hot air began moving slightly. A breeze was building, at last, swaying the palms, stirring the Spanish moss.

I sat on the porch in the dark and watched as heat lightning lit up whole scenes — of magnolias and oaks with Spanish moss blowing, of palms and orange trees. Long flickering sheets of light enveloped the porch and entered through the screens. Thunder rumbled on, distant and muffled.

*Beat the Heat Meals*

Summer is the time to enjoy light, cooling meals. Salads are a summer staple and refreshing drinks a blessing. We bake less in the summer and heat up the oven only when absolutely necessary.

# Memree's Soppin' Shrimp

*Memree makes a special trip to the Florida panhandle around Memorial Day and gets the fresh shrimp for this memorable meal.*

¼ pound butter
⅔ cup lemon juice
1 teaspoon grated lemon rind
1½ cups Italian dressing (see recipe)
2½ teaspoons black pepper, more to
   taste
3 pounds raw shrimp, in shell

Wash shrimp and remove heads, but leave in shell. Drain. In a medium saucepan, melt butter and add lemon juice, lemon rind, Italian dressing, and black pepper. Bring to a boil. Add shrimp and simmer for about 6 minutes or just until tender.

Serve with crusty French bread. Ladle shrimp into individual bowls with plenty of sauce for soppin' the bread in. You peel your own shrimp, which guarantees the pleasure of slow eating.

Serves 4.

# Orange Blush

1 cup fresh strawberries
4 cups orange juice
3 ice cubes

Mix fresh strawberries, orange juice, and ice cubes together in blender until smooth.

Serves 2.

# Dessie's Crab Enchalau

*To make this a full Spanish meal, serve with a Spanish salad, a dessert of guava shells in syrup, and very black coffee.*

1 dozen live blue crabs
1 gallon water
4 large bay leaves
2 tablespoons vinegar
1 tablespoon salt
¼ to ½ pound salt pork, diced fine
1 green pepper, chopped
½ pound onions, diced
2 cloves garlic, minced
¾ cup red wine
3 cups tomato puree
Salt and hot pepper, to taste

Keep blue crabs well-chilled on ice. In a large pot, combine water, 2 bay leaves, vinegar, and salt and bring to rolling boil. Drop crabs into boiling water and cook 3 minutes (they will start to turn orange). Don't overcook. They will have plenty of time to cook in the sauce. Reserving the liquid, remove the crabs from the pot and allow to cool. Crack the legs and clean the crab body.

Fry salt pork until crisp in a large Dutch oven. Remove from pot and use the grease to cook the green pepper, onions, and garlic. Add wine, tomato puree, 2 bay leaves, salt, and hot pepper to taste. Thin with crab juice until sauce resembles a thin spaghetti sauce. Cook one-half hour or longer — the longer the better. Add prepared crabs to the sauce and simmer for one-half hour to let the flavors blend well.

Serve crab and sauce in individual bowls. Dunk hot, buttered Cuban bread in the sauce and wear bibs!

Serves 6.

# Virginia's Eggplant Relish Salad

2 medium eggplants
1 teaspoon salt
½ cup olive oil
1½ pounds tomatoes
2 stalks celery
½ cup sliced black olives
2 tablespoons capers
1 tablespoon vinegar
1 teaspoon sugar or honey

Peel and dice eggplant. Sprinkle with salt. Let stand for 10 minutes. Blot with paper towel until dry, then brown in ¼ cup of the oil. Set aside.

Dice tomatoes and celery, and place in hot skillet with remaining oil. Cook over low heat for 15 minutes. Add olives, capers, vinegar, and sugar or honey. Cook 15 minutes more. Add eggplant and cook for 15 minutes. Taste for seasoning and adjust accordingly. Add more olives and capers if desired. Chill. May be used hot as a sauce or pizza topping.

Serves 6 as a salad.

# Avocado Halves

2 ripe avocados
4 teaspoons olive oil
4 teaspoons lemon juice
Soy sauce, to taste
Dash of cayenne (optional)

Cut avocados in half and remove pits. Combine remaining ingredients and spoon into each half.

Serves 4.

# Ginger Stir Fry

2 tablespoons cornstarch
2 tablespoons cooking oil
1 large sweet onion, halved and sliced
2 medium carrots, sliced
1 medium zucchini, cut in chunks
1 cup fresh broccoli, coarsely chopped
2 cups fresh spinach leaves
2 tablespoons fresh ginger, chopped
¾ cup water
¼ cup soy sauce
1 cake tofu (bean curd) cut in cubes

Mix cornstarch with water and soy sauce and set aside.

In a large skillet or wok, heat oil over high heat for 30 seconds. Add onion and carrots and cook, stirring constantly, for 3 minutes. Add zucchini and cook 2 minutes. Add broccoli and cook 2 minutes. Add spinach and cook 1 minute or just until softened. Add ginger and stir.

Push ingredients to one side. Pour cornstarch mixture into pan, stir until it thickens and clears, and mix all ingredients into sauce.

Gently fold in tofu cubes, heat through, and serve over hot rice.

Serves 4.

# Tacos Esoteric

½ cup each kidney beans, pinto beans,
  and black beans
6 cups water
3 tablespoons butter
3 cloves garlic, minced
1 cup diced onion
2 tablespoons minced jalapeno pepper
1 tablespoon lemon juice
Salt and pepper to taste

2 dozen smoked oysters
1 cup chopped black olives
1 cup sour cream
1 recipe Taco Sauce
1 cup shredded lettuce

12 corn tortillas
1 bottle hot sauce

Rinse beans and soak overnight. Drain and put in a large cooking pot with 6 cups water. Bring water to a boil, then turn down the heat, cover the pot, and simmer for 1 hour. Remove cover and cook the beans until tender. Drain beans and reserve the liquid.

In a large Dutch oven, heat butter and saute garlic, onion, and hot pepper until soft. Add beans, lemon juice, and enough bean liquid to cover. Bring to a simmer while you mash the beans with a potato masher. Cook for 15 minutes longer, stirring frequently, adding more bean liquid if necessary. Add salt and pepper to taste. These refried beans should be chunky and thick.

Heat tortillas and stack; cover with a cloth to keep them warm. Place on table with individual serving bowls of smoked oysters, olives, sour cream, taco sauce, shredded lettuce, and pot of refried beans.

Diners help themselves. Don't forget the hot sauce!

# Taco Sauce

1 cup sliced green onion
1 clove garlic, minced
3 medium tomatoes, diced
¼ cup Hot Pepper Vinegar (see recipe)
   or cider vinegar
¼ cup oil
¼ cup minced fresh parsley
1 teaspoon finely minced fresh
   coriander leaves (optional)

Mix together onion, garlic, and tomatoes. Add vinegar, oil, parsley, and coriander and stir well. For a smoother sauce, mix all ingredients in blender. Allow to stand at room temperature for 1 hour, stirring occasionally. Refrigerate in covered jar.

Makes 2 to 2½ cups.

# Tateroni Salad

15 to 18 medium potatoes, peeled and
    cut into small pieces
2 cups whole wheat or vegetable
    macaroni
1 cup broccoli heads, finely chopped
1 cup finely chopped onion
1 cup grated carrot
*Dressing*
1¼ cup plain low-fat yogurt
1 tablespoon spicy mustard
1 tablespoon mayonnaise
2 tablespoons sweet pickle relish
1 teaspoon whole celery seeds
2 medium garlic cloves, crushed
¼ cup finely chopped parsley
¼ teaspoon freshly grated black pepper

Steam or boil potatoes until just tender, about 15 to 20 minutes. Cook macaroni until al dente. Drain well.

In a large bowl, combine potatoes, macaroni, and vegetables and mix well. In a small bowl, combine dressing ingredients and mix well. Pour dressing over salad and toss. Chill at least 2 hours.

Serves 12 to 15.

# Steamy Summer Vegetables

*My "long hungry" friend Sean brought me a beautiful little fat-lighter'd pine spoon he had carved. Though the summer evening was hot and steamy, I was glad to cook this quick "beat the heat" meal in return for such a fine gift. The spoon was perfect for ladling the lemon-butter sauce over the steamed vegetables.*

2 cups sliced yellow squash (½-inch
    rounds)
2 cups sliced zucchini squash (½-inch
    rounds)
1 cup chopped green pepper
1 cup sliced onion
1 cup fresh corn
1 cup sliced tofu

*Lemon-butter sauce*
¼ cup melted butter, mixed with
2 tablespoons lemon juice

Place squash, green pepper, and onion on steaming basket in large saucepan. Add 1 inch of water to saucepan and bring to boil. Turn heat to low, cover pan, and simmer for 10 minutes or until squash is nearly tender. Cut corn off cob and add to other vegetables. Cook briefly until vegetables are tender, but still crisp.

Toss tofu with vegetables and pour lemon-butter sauce over them. Serve over brown rice or millet. Good with soy sauce.

Serves 4 to 6.

*Variations*
1. Instead of lemon-butter sauce, substitute ½ pound of grated sharp Cheddar cheese. Grate over hot vegetables and allow to melt.
2. Omit lemon-butter sauce and substitute butter pecan rice recipe for plain rice.

# Macaroni Salad con Verde

2 cups elbow macaroni
1 cup diced cooked ham
½ cup diced sweet red pepper
½ cup diced green pepper
¾ cup diced onion
½ cup diced celery
1 cup finely chopped broccoli
1 cup grated carrot

*Dressing*
½ cup olive oil
½ cup salad oil
4 medium cloves garlic, crushed
½ cup chopped fresh parsley
2 teaspoons chopped fresh basil or
　　1 teaspoon dried
2 teaspoons fresh oregano or 1 teaspoon
　　dried

Cook macaroni according to package directions. Drain.

In a large bowl, combine macaroni, ham, and chopped vegetables. Mix thoroughly. In a small bowl, mix dressing ingredients and beat with a whisk until well blended.

Pour dressing over salad, mix well, and chill for at least 2 hours. Serves 10.

# Tabouli

1 cup bulgur wheat
4 cups water
1 cup dried garbanzo beans
2 fresh mint leaves
¼ cup lemon juice
¼ cup olive oil
½ cup chopped parsley
½ cup chopped fresh mint
1 tablespoon chopped fresh basil
1 clove garlic, crushed
2 cups chopped fresh tomatoes
1 cup chopped green onions, with tops
½ teaspoon salt
½ teaspoon black pepper

Soak bulgur wheat overnight in 1 cup water. Soak garbanzo beans overnight in 3 cups water.

Combine beans with mint leaves in 2-quart saucepan and cook until tender. Mix together lemon juice, olive oil, parsley, mint, basil, garlic, tomato, and onion. Drain beans and marinate in the mixture for 2 hours at room temperature. Add salt and pepper to taste.

Serve as a salad in individual bowls or use as a filling for pita bread. Serves 3 or 4.

# Mexican Eggs

2 tablespoons butter
1 clove garlic, minced
½ cup diced onion
½ cup diced green pepper
½ cup diced tomato
¼ teaspoon cumin
2 teaspoons chopped fresh basil or
   ½ tsp. dried
8 eggs, beaten
½ teaspoon hot sauce (optional)
Salt and pepper to taste
8 tortillas

Melt butter in a 10-inch cast-iron skillet and saute garlic, onion, and green pepper. Add tomato, cumin, and basil. Simmer until vegetables are tender.

Pour beaten eggs into skillet and stir as for scrambled eggs until done. Add salt, pepper, and hot sauce as desired. Spoon onto hot tortillas and fold.

Serves 4.

# Chilled Tofu Salad

2 cakes tofu (8 oz. each), cut in cubes
¼ cup soy sauce
2 tablespoons grated fresh ginger
½ cup chopped scallions
3 tablespoons sesame seeds

In a medium bowl, mix tofu cubes and scallions. Mix soy sauce and ginger and pour over tofu, stirring gently. Chill 2 hours, mixing occasionally to coat tofu with marinade.

Serves 4.

Divide into 6 small bowls. Sprinkle each with 1 teaspoon sesame seeds.

Serves 6.

# Zucchini Bread

3 eggs
½ cup honey
½ cup oil
2 teaspoons vanilla
2 cups grated, unpeeled zucchini
2 tablespoons grated orange peel
3 cups whole wheat flour
1 teaspoon baking soda
¼ teaspoon baking powder
2 teaspoons cinnamon
½ cup raisins
½ cup pecans

Preheat oven to 325°. Beat eggs until light and fluffy. Add honey and beat well. Stir in oil, vanilla, zucchini, and orange peel.

Sift dry ingredients. Stir into liquid ingredients. Add raisins and nuts. Turn into 2 greased 8 x 4 loaf pans.

Bake at 325° for 50 to 60 minutes or until done. Cool on rack.

# Smoothies

A smoothie is a cool, refreshing beverage that is made in a blender. It has as a base either fruit juice, yogurt, or milk. Fresh fruits in season are added to flavor and thicken the drink, and ice cubes may be added to chill it. All ingredients should be well blended. The variations are infinite. And the result, in a tall glass, is especially refreshing on a hot summer day.

You can make a cold smoothie without ice cubes by freezing the fruits in advance in air-tight plastic containers. To prepare for freezing, hull strawberries and cut into chunks; peel bananas and sprinkle with a little lemon juice to prevent darkening; mash the persimmon pulp. When ready to use the persimmon pulp, remove from container and cut into chunks. Or freeze whole persimmons with the peel; once frozen, the peel can be slivered off easily with a knife without taking any of the pulp.

*Suggestions for Summer Smoothies*

Fruit juice base — use orange juice, pineapple juice, or apple juice.

Fruits — bananas, strawberries, pineapple, cantaloupe, or peaches, alone or in combination.

For added flavor — freeze lemon or orange juice in ice cube trays and add one or two cubes to bring out the flavor of other juices and fruits.

# Persimmon Lime Freeze

1 cup frozen persimmon pulp
3 tablespoons lime juice
3 cups water
¼ cup honey, or more to taste
2 or 3 ice cubes

In the fall when persimmons are ripe, peel them and freeze the pulp in 1-cup plastic containers. When ready to use, remove pulp from container and cut into 1-inch chunks.

Combine persimmon pulp, lime juice, and water in blender. Add honey a little at a time while blending so it will dissolve. Then add ice cubes and blend until smooth.

Serves 2.


# Doug's Strawberry Sunset Drink

3 cups cranberry juice
1¼ cup ripe strawberries
   (or unsweetened frozen)
6 ounces vanilla yogurt

Cut fresh strawberries into chunks and freeze overnight or until ready to use. Break up frozen strawberries and put into blender. Add vanilla yogurt and cranberry juice. Blend until smooth. Makes 1 quart.

Pour into tall glasses. Walk out onto the porch, put your feet up, and enjoy a summer sunset.

Note: If it's a hot day and you can't wait for strawberries to freeze, use fresh strawberries and a few ice cubes.

# Refreshing Pineapple Mint

2 tablespoons finely chopped, fresh
   mint
3 cups pineapple juice
½ cup lemon juice
Honey, if desired
4 ice cubes

Mix mint with ½ cup pineapple juice in blender. Then add rest of pineapple juice, lemon juice, and ice cubes and blend well until mint is dissolved. Serve in tall glasses with fresh sprig of mint, a pineapple chunk, or lemon slice.

Serves 2.


# Lemon Banana Beverage

1 banana, sliced
⅓ cup lemon juice
1 tablespoon honey (or more, to taste)
⅓ cup plain yogurt
3 ice cubes (if using frozen banana,
   eliminate ice cubes)

Place banana, lemon juice, and honey in blender and mix until honey is dissolved. Add yogurt and ice cubes and blend well.

Makes about 1 cup.

# Creamy Orange Drink

1 cup yogurt or buttermilk
4 ice cubes
4 cups orange juice
1 sliced banana (optional)

Put yogurt in blender. Add ice cubes, then orange juice. Blend until smooth and creamy.

Blend in sliced bananas for a thicker, sweeter drink.

Serves 2 to 4.

## Heat-Hardy Fruits and Vegetables

The heat-hardy fruits that survive the tropical Florida summers reward us for persevering through the months of heat. Blueberries ripen wild in the pinewoods and are cultivated locally. Kate and I pick our berries at a nearby U-Pick-Em berry patch. The owner picks right along with us, laughing at a young child who can't stop eating the sweet berries and grinning at our blue-stained teeth. The morning starts cool, with a light breeze off the lake, but as the heat and humidity build, we watch for rain. Once we heard the distant thunder of the space shuttle taking off. We fill our buckets, then seek a nearby lake for a refreshing dip.

# Blueberry Yogurt Muffins

1 cup unbleached white flour
½ cup cornmeal
½ cup whole wheat flour
1 teaspoon baking powder
½ teaspoon baking soda
½ teaspoon nutmeg
1¼ cups plain yogurt
1 egg, beaten
⅓ cup honey or maple syrup
1 teaspoon finely grated lemon peel
1 cup blueberries

Preheat oven to 425°. Sift dry ingredients together. Combine liquid ingredients and stir into dry ingredients. Add lemon peel. Fold in blueberries.

Fill greased muffin tins one-half full. Bake at 425° for 15 to 20 minutes or until done.

Makes 10 to 12 muffins.


# Blueberry Pecan Cobbler

2 tablespoons cornstarch
1 teaspoon cinnamon
2 tablespoons sugar
6 cups fresh blueberries (or frozen)
1 cup coarsely chopped pecans
¼ cup butter
½ cup maple syrup or honey

Grease an 8 x 8 baking dish. Mix together cornstarch, cinnamon and sugar. Add blueberries and stir until all are coated. Pour into baking dish and sprinkle pecans evenly over top.

Melt butter in a small saucepan. Mix in syrup or honey until blended. Spoon over pecans.

Bake at 350° about 30 minutes or until bubbly and browned. Serve warm with whipped cream or yogurt sweetened with maple syrup.

Serves 6.

In August, my neighbor Jane calls me up and reminds me, "The pears are ready." The fullness of summer has rolled around again and provided a good excuse for getting together.

I drive around Orange Lake to her old two-story cracker home, surrounded by large pecan and citrus trees. Walking past quietly grazing cows, I set my ladder in the pear tree. A warm breeze blows across the sloping pasture as I pick the pears and marvel that summer is already half over. Jane invites me inside, and we sit in the cool kitchen sampling her freshly baked pear cobbler. Jars of seasonal preserves crowd the cupboard shelves, and on the counter is a tall stack of recipes that we leaf through leisurely.

# Jane's Florida Pear Cobbler

*Pear sauce*
5 medium pears
2 cups water
¼ cup honey
½ teaspoon cinnamon
½ teaspoon nutmeg
¼ teaspoon ginger
*Dough*
¼ pound margarine
¾ cup whole wheat flour
½ teaspoon salt
2 teaspoons baking powder
¾ cup milk
½ cup honey

Peel pears, cut into quarters, and core. Chop coarsely. Place in medium saucepan with water, honey, and spices. Simmer until tender and slightly thickened. This makes 2 generous cups of pear chunks.

Preheat oven to 350°. Melt margarine in 2-quart casserole. Sift flour, baking powder, and salt together in medium bowl. Heat milk in small saucepan and add honey, stirring until dissolved. Pour liquid into flour mixture gradually, stirring to remove lumps. Batter will be thin. Pour over melted margarine in casserole. Then spoon pears and juice by tablespoons into batter. Bake at 350° about 45 minutes or until done.

Makes 9 servings.

# Mike's Pear Pecan Pie

½ cup brown sugar
1½ tablespoons cornstarch
1 teaspoon cinnamon
½ teaspoon nutmeg
¼ teaspoon cloves
¼ teaspoon ginger
6 cups fresh pear slices, peeled
1 cup chopped pecans
2 tablespoons butter
Pastry for a 2-crust pie

Preheat oven to 450°. Line a 9-inch pie pan with pastry. Mix cornstarch with brown sugar and spices. Mix with pear slices. Arrange in layers in pie shell with pecans between layers. Dot top with butter.

Cover with upper crust and prick a few holes in the top.

Bake at 450° for 10 minutes. Reduce heat to 350° and bake until done, about 45 minutes.

# Memree's Pear-A-Dice Cake

1½ cups unbleached white flour
1½ cups whole wheat flour
Pinch salt
1 teaspoon baking soda
1¼ cups corn oil
1 cup light wildflower honey (gallberry
    preferred)
2 teaspoons vanilla
3 eggs, well beaten
3 cups coarsely chopped pear or apple,
    unpeeled
1 cup chopped nuts

In a large bowl, sift together flours, salt, and baking soda. In a small bowl, mix oil, honey, and vanilla with eggs. Add liquid ingredients to dry, and blend in pears and nuts.

Pour into a greased 9 x 12 baking pan. Place pan in unheated oven and set for 325°. Bake 45 minutes or until knife inserted in center comes out clean.

This cake is usually served unfrosted, but a good frosting can be made by mixing:
½ cup butter, creamed
1 cup light brown sugar
1 cup evaporated milk
1 teaspoon vanilla

# Pear Butter

5 pounds pears
¼ cup lemon juice
Honey, to taste
2 teaspoons cinnamon
1 teaspoon allspice
½ teaspoon cloves
1 teaspoon grated lemon peel

Wash pears and cut into quarters. Remove core, but do not peel. Cut into small chunks and place in large enamel or stainless steel saucepan with lemon juice and water to cover. Cook over low heat until soft, stirring occasionally. Press through coarse sieve.

Measure pulp and return to pan. Taste for sweetness and add honey (¼ to ½ cup for each cup of pear pulp.) Add spices and lemon rind. Cook slowly, stirring constantly until thick. Follow standard canning process for storage, or make a small batch for immediate use. (Important: contact your county extension office home economist or consult USDA bulletin #56 for complete and safe canning instructions.)

Makes 1½ to 2 quarts.

Wild plums ripen in shades of scarlet, yellow-gold, purple, and clear red. The wild plum jam I make is coveted by my friends Allie and Sam, who casually mention their upcoming birthdays while eyeing the golden or burgundy jars. They promise that one jar is all they could ever want for a gift. This year I gave them their own plum tree.

# Wild Plum Jam

2½ pounds plums
2 cups mild honey

Wash the plums, admiring all their different colors — purple, scarlet, and golden orange. Simmer in water just to cover, until skins are tender. Cool, then remove the pits.

Measure 4 cups of plum pulp into a 2-quart enamel or stainless steel saucepan. Bring to a full boil. Add 2 cups of honey, stirring until dissolved. Taste for sweetness and add more honey if desired. It is important not to over-sweeten, so that the true plum flavor will dominate.

Continue boiling, stirring constantly until mixture thickens. Follow standard canning process for storage, or make a smaller batch for immediate use. (Important: contact your county extension office home economist or consult USDA bulletin #56 for complete and safe canning instructions.)

Makes 5 or 6 half-pint jars.

I enjoy exclusive rights to the fig crop on Kate and Gary's two backyard fig trees while they are in the Carolinas for the summer. I tempt them with long letters describing the luscious concoctions the bounty yields. The small sugar figs and large black turkey figs feed the birds and wasps, the raccoons and me. If none of us has been too greedy, there is plenty for all — even a jar or two of fig preserves for Kate and Gary at summer's end.

# Lemon Rice Fig Custard

2 tablespoons butter
¼ cup honey
3 eggs, beaten
2 cups milk
3 tablespoons lemon juice
1 cup cooked brown rice
1 cup chopped fresh figs
2 tablespoons lemon rind
½ teaspoon nutmeg
½ teaspoon cinnamon

Melt butter in small saucepan. Add honey, stirring until dissolved. Beat eggs, and blend together with milk and lemon juice. Mix in butter and honey until well blended.

Combine rice, figs, and lemon rind with 1 cup of custard mixture. Pour into a buttered 2-quart round pan. Pour in the rest of the custard. Sprinkle with nutmeg and cinnamon.

Bake at 325° over a pan of water for about 45 minutes or until firm.

# Spicy Fig Preserves

4 cups chopped fresh figs
3 cups water
1 teaspoon each cinnamon, ginger,
    and ground cloves
1 tablespoon finely grated lemon peel
Honey to taste (about ½ cup)

Wash figs and drain. Cut off stem ends. Chop figs and put in large pot with water. Add spices and lemon peel and simmer gently for 30 minutes, or until the mixture begins to thicken. Add honey to taste. Stir and cook until thick. Follow standard canning process for storage, or make a small batch for immediate use. (Important: contact your county extension office home economist or consult USDA bulletin #56 for complete and safe canning instructions.)

Makes about 2 cups.

Note: You may substitute dried figs for fresh, in which case use slightly more water.

There are some vegetables that not only survive the heat but that actually thrive on sultry days and humid nights. One of my favorite summer vegetables is okra, whose pretty cream-colored flower has a red velvet center. Though often scoffed at as slimy, this underrated vegetable maintains its texture and flavor when prepared properly.

One summer my neighbor Leo raised an exceptional patch of okra. The plants grew quickly, and by summer's end the stalks stood eight and ten feet tall. The pods seemed to grow overnight, so

I helped to harvest them before they grew tough or fibrous. Again and again, I filled my basket with tender pods no larger than three inches. Within the week, I had canned twenty-four quarts, sure that this would be plenty for family and friends. The only thing that got me through the hot canning process was knowing how good the chilled pickles would taste. After they had seasoned a few months, the pickled okra became one of the favorite items in my walk-in pantry, and all twenty-four quarts were gone before the year was over.

# Pickled Okra

7 cloves garlic
7 hot peppers
¼ bushel small okra (1″ to 3″),
   scrubbed (about 3 lbs.)
7 sprigs dill
1 quart distilled white vinegar
1 cup water
½ teaspoon salt (pure granulated
   or kosher)

Sterilize 7 pint jars. While still hot, place 1 clove garlic, 1 sprig dill, and 1 hot pepper in the bottom of each jar. Pack with okra.

Bring vinegar, water, and salt to boil and simmer 5 minutes. Pour immediately over okra. Follow standard canning process. (Important: contact your county extension office home economist or consult USDA bulletin #92 for complete and safe canning instructions.)

Makes 5 pints.

Whenever I make okra creole, I'm reminded of an evening when I served it to a few friends at the Rawlings house. The night was tropical; a soft breeze picked up at dark and stirred the cabbage palms. Crickets hummed on the night air. A single lantern illumined the round wood table where we sat on deerhide chairs. The road was quiet, and a barred owl called. I served the creole with cornbread, white wine, and, for dessert, pear-pecan pie.

# Okra Creole

1 3-pound chicken
2 bay leaves
2 tablespoons oil
2 garlic cloves, minced
1 cup chopped onion
1 cup chopped green pepper
2 cups chopped fresh tomato
1 tablespoon minced fresh basil or
    1 teaspoon dried
2 teaspoons minced fresh thyme or
    ¼ teaspoon dried
¼ teaspoon chili powder
1 teaspoon black pepper
1 teaspoon salt
3 cups chicken broth
3 cups sliced okra (in ½-inch rounds)
1 teaspoon Hot Pepper Vinegar (see recipe)
Hot Pepper Sauce to taste (see recipe) or
    cider vinegar
1 pound medium shrimp, shelled and
    deveined

Place chicken and bay leaves in large saucepan with water to cover and simmer until tender. Remove chicken and allow to cool. Remove skin and cut chicken into bite-size pieces.

In 3-quart Dutch oven, heat oil and saute garlic, onions, and green peppers until soft. Add tomato, basil, thyme, chili powder, pepper, salt, and chicken broth and simmer for 10 minutes. Add chicken pieces, okra, Hot Pepper Vinegar, and Hot Pepper Sauce. Simmer 15 minutes or until okra is tender. Add shrimp and cook just until done. Serve hot over lemon rice (see recipe).

Serves 6 to 8.

A visitor set up her easel in the yard and began painting the Rawlings home. There were no other visitors all morning, so I busied myself weeding the garden. Her voice at the garden gate startled me. "Do you grow these vegetables yourself?" she asked. "Yes," I assured her. "And you eat them, too?" she wanted to know. "Yes," I responded and invited her to join me for a bowl of garden gazpacho. I had already picked the tomatoes, cucumbers, onions, and green peppers, since the ingredients for this cold vegetable soup must be finely chopped and the flavors allowed to blend at room temperature a few hours.

# Gusty Gazpacho

4 cups diced tomato
2 cloves garlic, minced
1 cup sliced cucumber
1 cup chopped green pepper
1 cup sliced green onion
¼ cup olive oil
¼ cup cider vinegar
¼ cup lemon juice
2 teaspoons soy sauce
2 teaspoons paprika
1 teaspoon black pepper
Hot sauce to taste

Combine tomato, garlic, cucumber, green pepper, and onion in large mixing bowl. Mix together olive oil, vinegar, lemon juice, soy sauce, paprika, and black pepper and pour over vegetables. Add hot sauce, if desired.

Mix well and let stand at room temperature for 1 hour, stirring frequently. Cover and chill in refrigerator at least 2 hours.

Serves 6.

The eggplant's glossy purple sheen glows from among the garden greenery all summer long. There are many who find its beauty only skin-deep, however, and consider it bland and tasteless. No wonder, with recipes that call for salting it, soaking it, and cooking it in oil, which it then absorbs in large quantities.

One secret to optimum taste is to select young eggplant before they become too large and bitter. Treat them gently. The pretty purple skin bruises easily.

# Stuffed Eggplant

2 medium eggplants
2 teaspoons butter
1 medium onion, chopped
1 clove garlic, minced
1 teaspoon chopped fresh basil or
    ½ teaspoon dried
1 teaspoon chopped fresh majoram or
    ½ teaspoon dried
½ teaspoon chopped fresh thyme or
    ¼ teaspoon dried
1 cup cooked corn kernels
2 cups cooked brown rice
1 cup grated sharp Cheddar cheese

Remove stem ends from eggplant and cut in half lengthwise. Scoop out and dice insides, leaving a ¼-inch shell.

Melt butter in a 10-inch skillet and saute onion and diced eggplant until tender. Stir in garlic and herbs. Stir in corn and rice and heat through.

Pile mixture into shells. Top each with ¼ cup cheese. Place shells in a shallow pan in ¼ inch of water. Bake at 375° for 45 minutes.

Serves 4.

# Allie's Eggplant Pie

Pastry for 2-crust pie
1 eggplant, peeled, cut into ⅓-inch slices
¾ cup olive or vegetable oil
1 large onion, sliced thin
1 green pepper, halved and cut into thin
    strips
1 zucchini squash, sliced
2 cloves garlic, minced
¾ teaspoon oregano
¾ teaspoon basil
½ teaspoon salt
½ teaspoon black pepper
½ cup grated Parmesan cheese
2 large tomatoes, cut into ⅛-inch
    wedges
8 ounces Mozzarella cheese, grated

Prepare pastry. Roll and fit one-half into 10-inch pie plate. Refrigerate, along with remaining ball of pastry.

Cut eggplant slices into ⅓-inch cubes. Heat ½ cup oil in large cast-iron skillet. Add eggplant all at once and quickly toss to coat with oil. Cook, stirring constantly, until eggplant is just tender — about 5 minutes. Remove to large bowl.

Heat remaining oil (¼ cup) in skillet. Add onion, green pepper, zucchini, and garlic. Cook and stir until vegetables are just tender, but have not lost their shape, about 5 minutes. Remove to a separate bowl. Combine oregano, basil, salt, and pepper in a small cup.

Preheat oven to 425°. Remove pastry from refrigerator; sprinkle bottom of pie with 3 tablespoons grated Parmesan cheese. Spoon one-half the eggplant over cheese, then add half the vegetable mixture. Arrange one-half the tomato wedges over vegetables, sprinkle with half the herbs, 1 tablespoon Parmesan cheese, and half the Mozzarella cheese. Repeat layers with the remaining ingredients, reserving 1 table-spoon Parmesan cheese.

Roll out remaining pastry. Cut into ½-inch strips and arrange in lattice-fashion over the pie. Trim strips and fit to bottom pastry. Brush with milk (or water). Sprinkle with remaining Parmesan cheese.

Bake in 425° oven for 25 to 30 minutes or until pastry is golden brown and pie is just beginning to bubble. Let cool a little — 10 minutes or so — before cutting.

Makes 8 servings.

*Fourth of July*

By the Fourth of July, we know for certain that summer is upon us. We play games of volleyball and horseshoes through the long, hot afternoon. Someone usually suggests a drive to the limerock quarry for a swim. We return to Kate and Gary's house and spread quilts and blankets on the grass in the shade of pine trees. The tables are soon crowded with everyone's casserole dishes. Hungry after a day of strenuous games, we appreciate our ample picnic.

# Ted's Herb-Smoked Turkey

3 cups hickory chips
30 to 40 charcoal briquets
6 pieces bacon, chopped
2 large cloves garlic, minced or pressed
4 tablespoons butter
½ cup chopped fresh parsley
2 tablespoons rubbed sage
2 tablespoons dried thyme
1  20-pound turkey
2 tablespoons melted butter
1 teaspoon freshly ground black pepper
4 strips bacon

Soak hickory chips in water overnight. About 5 hours before serving time, light charcoal in a large barbecue grill with domed cover. When fire is ready, place pan of water in center of evenly distributed charcoal and adjust grill about 6 inches above coals.

Combine chopped bacon, garlic, parsley, butter, and herbs and rub in cavity of turkey. Tie legs together with string. Baste top of turkey with melted butter, sprinkle with pepper, and place bacon strips over the skin. Secure bacon by wrapping bird with string.

Place turkey on grill, cover, and cook 1½ hours. Begin adding hickory chips a few at a time and replace charcoal and water as needed.

Continue cooking and adding hickory chips for another 2 hours. Remove bacon strips. Continue cooking until turkey is browned and thigh meat springs back when pressed with fork, about ½ hour. (Total cooking time is about 4 hours.)

# Barbecued Chicken

4 chicken breasts, cut in half
4 cups water
1 cup Ginger-Lemon or Key Lime
   Barbecue Sauce (see recipe)

Remove skin from chicken. Place chicken in a large skillet, add water to cover, and cover skillet. Bring to boil and simmer for 20 minutes.

Remove chicken from stock and while still hot, baste liberally with barbecue sauce. This can be done 1 to 3 hours before barbeque time.

Prepare a charcoal fire with the grill about 6 inches above the coals. Grill chicken for about 15 minutes, turning and basting frequently, until nicely browned. Don't overcook as this will cause the chicken to dry out.

Serves 4 to 6.

# Bev's Festive Rice Salad

1½ cups uncooked brown rice
3 cups chicken broth
8-ounce jar marinated artichoke hearts
⅓ cup mayonnaise
¼ teaspoon curry powder
4 to 6 green onions with tops, chopped
4 ounces pimento-stuffed green olives,
   sliced

Cook rice in chicken broth. Drain artichoke hearts, reserving liquid. Mix mayonnaise, curry powder, and artichoke liquid.

Chop artichoke hearts and combine with rice and other ingredients in a large bowl; blend well. Refrigerate until well chilled.

Serves 6.

# Gert's Baked Beans

1 pound (2 cups) dried pea beans
½ pound salt pork with rind
1 cup light brown sugar (or ⅔ cup cane
    syrup)
1 teaspoon salt
¼ cup granulated sugar

Wash beans. Place in a heavy pot with water to cover and soak overnight.

Cut salt pork into ¼-inch slices down to the rind. Add to the water and beans. Add the brown sugar and salt and boil until the beans begin to soften (not mushy).

Remove salt pork and place beans in a 7 x 10 x 2 baking dish. Arrange pork in neat rows on top of the beans. Sprinkle with granulated sugar.

Cover and bake in a slow oven (300° or 325°) about 4 hours. Remove cover during last ½ hour of baking to let beans brown. Such a racy, tantalizing aroma!

Serves 6 to 8.

# Angie's Carrot-Pineapple Salad

2 medium carrots, grated
¼ cup crushed pineapple, drained
¼ cup chopped pecans or walnuts
¼ cup raisins
2 tablespoons lemon juice
½ teaspoon grated lemon rind
½ cup plain yogurt

Mix all ingredients in a medium bowl. Chill at least 2 hours.
Makes 6 to 8 servings.

# Sweet Potato Salad

4 cups diced cooked sweet potatoes
1½ cups sliced green onions, with tops
1 cup diced green pepper
¼ cup mayonnaise
1 teaspoon vinegar
½ teaspoon black pepper
Salt to taste

In a medium bowl mix together sweet potatoes, onions, green pepper, mayonnaise, vinegar, and black pepper. Salt to taste. Add a little more vinegar if desired. For a creamy texture, the sweet potatoes may be mashed while stirring, but leave some of the potatoes in chunks, too!


# Betty's Squash Casserole

10 to 12 medium yellow squash, sliced
1 large onion, chopped
8 ounces sharp Cheddar cheese, grated
¼ cup butter or margarine
1 cup herb-seasoned stuffing
Salt and pepper to taste

Steam the squash and onion until just tender. Drain well. In large bowl, mix together squash, onion, cheese, butter, one-half stuffing mix, and salt and pepper to taste.

Pour into 8 x 12 casserole. Sprinkle other half of stuffing mix on top. Bake at 350° for 30 minutes or until light brown.

Serves 6 to 8.

Note: May substitute some zucchini squash for added color and flavor.

# Eileen's Onion-Zucchini Bread

3 cups unbleached white flour
¾ cup chopped onions
½ cup Parmesan cheese
5 teaspoons baking powder
½ teaspoon baking soda
⅓ cup salad oil
1 cup buttermilk
2 eggs, beaten
¾ cup grated zucchini

Preheat oven to 350°. Combine flour, onion, 6 tablespoons Parmesan cheese, baking powder, and baking soda in a medium bowl.

In a small bowl, mix together salad oil, buttermilk, eggs, and zucchini.

Stir liquid ingredients into dry. Spoon into a greased 9- or 10-inch round baking pan. Sprinkle with remaining Parmesan cheese. Bake at 350° for 45 to 50 minutes or until knife inserted in center comes out clean. Cool 10 minutes before removing from pan.

Makes 12 servings.

# Ginger-Lemon Barbecue Sauce

1 tablespoon butter
1 large green onion, diced
1 tablespoon chopped fresh ginger
¾ cup catsup
½ cup water
2 tablespoons Worcestershire sauce
3 tablespoons brown sugar
3 tablespoons lemon juice
1 tablespoon grated lemon rind
½ teaspoon allspice

In a small saucepan, melt butter and saute green onion and ginger for 1 minute. Add all other ingredients; bring to a boil and simmer gently for 10 minutes.

This sauce is ideal for chicken and can be used both as a marinade and a basting sauce for barbecue.


# Key Lime Barbecue Sauce

2 or 3 key limes
1 tablespoon butter
1 small onion, finely chopped
2 small cloves garlic, minced
1½ cups catsup
3 tablespoons red wine vinegar
6 tablespoons honey
3 tablespoons Worcestershire sauce
1 tablespoon prepared mustard

Grate rind from limes, then cut the limes in half and squeeze juice into a small bowl and set aside.

In a medium saucepan, melt butter and saute onion until transparent, about 2 minutes. Add lime rind and garlic and saute 1 minute. Add the rest of ingredients; bring to boil and simmer gently for 10 minutes.

Marinate chickens for one hour in this sauce before barbecuing. Baste with sauce as needed.

# Independent Blueberry Pie

5 cups fresh blueberries
⅔ cup sugar
3½ tablespoons cornstarch
2 tablespoons lemon juice
1 tablespoon grated lemon rind
½ teaspoon cinnamon
½ teaspoon nutmeg
¼ teaspoon allspice
Pastry for 2-crust pie

Line a 10-inch pie pan with crust.

Mix blueberries with cornstarch, sugar, lemon juice, lemon rind, and spices. Allow to stand 15 minutes, then mix again. Pour into crust and cover with top crust. Pierce in several places.

Bake in a 450° oven for 10 minutes, then reduce heat to 350° and bake 40 to 45 minutes.

Serves 8.

We finish eating at dusk, and as stars begin to show, it's time for fireworks. The rockets, flares, and sparklers elicit appreciative "oohs" and "aahs." After the last light from the grand finale burns out, we admire the bright display of stars in the clear night sky.

*Beach Picnics*

There's a sense of adventure in leaving for the beach in the early morning dark. It has been a long time since I've seen the sun rise over the ocean. While we are driving to the beach, past palmetto thickets and cabbage palms, the moon sets. We reach the ocean before sunrise. I can't quite make out the forms, but I can hear the shorebirds skittering along the wet edge of the ocean. The water is warm and calm, as though still asleep, and we swim while the sun rises.

Suddenly, wave crests are touched with mauve, lavender, and rose. The colors blend and change as the waves roll, and we watch the sun drop a glittering yellow line through it all. Schools of silver mullet swim with us, and brown pelicans in formation fly low and gracefully over the water. Three porpoises roll through the waves; their slow-rocking backs cut across the sun's yellow trail one by one. We spend the morning catching mullet and then, sunburned, salty, and tired, enjoy frying our catch over an open fire.

# Mullet

*"Umm, umm, umm, indeed a delicacy, a succulent delight!"* My friend *Richard becomes enthusiastic at just the mention of mullet, and has been known to catch his share. He fillets the mullet expertly with a sharp knife and stresses that mullet must be cleaned and washed thoroughly. "The secret to this recipe is heat!" he exclaims. "The oil must be smoking ... ready to burst into flame. Throw mullet into super-hot grease and it makes a shattering sound. Ah, the smell! Instantly the batter is golden. The succulent meat inside is unscathed and steamed. Ecstasy!"*

1½ cups cooking oil
2 pounds mullet fillets
1 cup cornmeal
1 cup unbleached white flour
½ teaspoon salt
½ teaspoon black pepper

Slice fillets into serving size pieces. Mix cornmeal, flour, salt, and pepper. Roll mullet in cornmeal coating. Heat oil in 10-inch cast-iron skillet. Drop fish into hot oil. Cook at moderate heat for 3 to 4 minutes or until brown. Turn and brown on other side. Fish is done when it flakes easily with a fork. Drain on absorbent paper and serve hot with lemon wedges.

Serve 4 to 6.

# Corn Fritters

4 ears of corn (or 2 cups kernels),
   uncooked
3 eggs, beaten
Pepper to taste
1 tablespoon butter, more as needed

In a medium bowl mix corn cut from cob, pepper, and beaten eggs.

Melt butter in 10-inch skillet. For each individual fritter, drop 2 tablespoons corn mixture into hot skillet. Flatten into thin cake and brown quickly on one side. Turn and brown on other side.

These are good plain or may be served with cane syrup or honey. Makes 8.

Sometimes we go to the beach in the evening to avoid spending a full day in the blistering sun. We dig a fire pit in the sand, gather driftwood, and start the fire. While waiting for a good bed of coals, we take an evening swim as the sun sets, and a warm ocean breeze picks up. A great blue heron stands in the shallows, a gaunt shadow in the dusk.

When the coals are ready we cook grouper in a cast-iron pan with butter and lemon. Sweet potatoes tucked in the coals bake slowly while we toss a fresh green salad. Blueberry muffins brown in our camping oven, and there's wine, coffee, and dessert after a moonlight walk. Salty waves beat a soothing rhythm against the sand where embedded shells glisten in the moonlight.

# Beach Grouper

2 pounds grouper fillets
2 tablespoons butter
¼ cup lemon juice
½ teaspoon tarragon
⅓ cup fresh minced parsley

Cut grouper into 3-inch pieces. Melt butter in large cast-iron skillet and brown grouper on one side. Turn, brown on other side and add lemon juice, tarragon, and parsley. Cover and cook until fish flakes easily with a fork.

Serves 4.

# End of Summer Fruit Salad

*Pear slices, persimmon wedges, and grapes simmered with lemon and honey are proof of the compatibility of fruits grown in the same season. They make an unforgettable blend of spicy perfection.*

5 pears, with peel
2 persimmons, peeled
1 small bunch of grapes
¼ cup lemon juice
¼ cup honey

Slice pears into a 2-quart saucepan. Add persimmons, cut into wedges, and grapes cut into halves with seeds removed. Pour lemon juice and honey over fruit and simmer briefly on low, stirring to prevent sticking. Do not overcook — the pears should retain their texture. Add a little water if necessary.

Serves 4 to 5.

Note: These fruits are also good together uncooked, with just a little lemon juice sprinkled over them.

*Hot Peppers*

One day an elderly woman and her husband walked into the Rawlings kitchen. The woman picked up a bottle of Datil pepper sauce, exclaiming, "I haven't seen any of this in years. Is it for sale?" When I replied negatively, she was crestfallen. I offered the couple some seeds, and her husband accepted gratefully. Then I noticed how frail and old they were; they would never be able to plant a garden and grow their own. I had two bottles, and the large one was really enough for me. I gave her the smaller bottle, and, in gratitude, she traded me her secret for making pilau.

*Pilau Secret*

Add 1 to 2 teaspoons Hot Pepper Vinegar to cooked rice. This really brings out the flavor.

# Cross Creek Hot Pepper Sauce

4 dozen Datil peppers or any small,
   hot peppers
1 clove garlic, minced
1 teaspoon honey
¼ cup cider vinegar

Wash peppers and remove stem ends. Simmer peppers and garlic in medium saucepan with water to cover, until tender. Press through a fine sieve and return to saucepan. Add honey and vinegar. Stir and simmer briefly until well blended.

Makes approximately 1 to 1½ cups.

Hot peppers make a colorful addition to any garden with their green, red, yellow, and orange hues. They range from the mild banana peppers to the hottest Datil peppers, which retain the heat of Florida's summer sun. Hot peppers will grow on through the fall and even through a mild winter if there are no freezes.

# Allie's Chiles Rellenos

12 to 15 fresh, hot Hungarian banana
    peppers
2½ cups grated Monterey Jack cheese
3 eggs, beaten
1½ cups milk

Preheat oven to 350°. Cut tops off peppers and make a lengthwise slit on one side. For a mild version, remove seeds. The more seeds you leave, the hotter the final result. (I usually remove the membranes and lightly rinse the inside of the peppers, leaving approximately one-fourth to one-third of the seeds).

Stuff the peppers with grated cheese, retaining some cheese for topping. Place peppers seam-down in ungreased casserole. Beat eggs and milk together and pour over peppers until almost, but not quite, covered. Sprinkle top with any leftover cheese.

Bake at 350° until puffed and firm and slightly browned (approximately 35 to 45 minutes). Serve with Mexican Cornbread (see recipe).

Serves 4.

Hot Pepper vinegar is one of the simplest hot pepper recipes and it is a southern requisite for cooked greens. I've been told that the vinegar helps the body assimilate the vitamins in the greens. Whether or not this is true, it definitely enhances the flavor. Anyone can make his own supply in a matter of minutes.

## Hot Pepper Vinegar

Fill an empty wine, whiskey, soda pop, or ketchup bottle with fresh hot peppers. Pour apple cider vinegar over the peppers to cover. The vinegar may be heated, but this isn't necessary. Seal with a cork. The vinegar improves with age. You may continue replenishing the vinegar as it's used up. Use mild or hot peppers according to your preference, or a combination of the two.

# 7. Fall

The wind and the leaves take up the talking, and pecans fall steadily through the tranquil fall days. I count six eagles soaring overhead on the wind. The clucking of the chickens in the distance sounds like human voices, and I try to make out what they are saying. Fruits are ripening outside every window. The oranges are beginning to earn their name now; I watch them expectantly, almost anxiously, for some are still so dark green that I think they'll never turn orange. The tea olive is blooming again; little hints of heady fragrance seek me out when I least expect it. The swaying tops of lanky cabbage palms fill me with childlike awe. I reflect on my childhood when everything was taller and I was continually looking up, and the world was something to wonder about.

The pecan trees in the Rawlings grove usually bear a good crop every other year. We harvest the nuts in the fall and store them in the pantry for a few weeks to improve their flavor. Then, while sitting by the fire, or on the porch during a rain, we shell the pecans. We save some for pies and freeze the rest to last through the year.

The sweet, nutty flavor of pecans makes them an excellent snack just plain, or mixed with other fresh nuts. Pecans make a versatile topping for casseroles, pies, and cobblers. Try them in granola or fruit salads; with rice or stir-fries.

# Gary's Butter Pecan Bread

½ cup coarsely chopped pecans
10 to 12 pecan halves
2 teaspoons butter
½ teaspoon sugar
¼ teaspoon garlic salt
2 cups whole wheat flour, sifted
2 teaspoons baking powder
½ teaspoon salt
½ cup butter or margarine
½ cup milk
1 egg, slightly beaten
¼ cup maple syrup or cane syrup
1 tablespoon sesame seeds

Preheat oven to 350°. Melt butter in a small skillet and toast pecans until lightly browned. Remove from heat, stir in sugar and garlic salt, and set aside.

In a medium bowl, combine flour, baking powder, and salt. Cut in butter or margarine until mixture resembles coarse crumbs. In a small bowl, combine milk, egg, and syrup, mixing well. Add wet ingredients to dry and blend until moist. Stir in chopped pecans and sesame seeds.

Spread mixture evenly in a greased 8 x 8 pan or cast iron skillet. Press pecan halves into top. Bake at 350° for 45 minutes or until golden brown.

# Orange Pecan Coffee Cake

3 cups whole wheat flour
2 teaspoons baking powder
1 teaspoon baking soda
1 teaspoon cinnamon
2 tablespoons grated orange peel
1 cup chopped pecans
2 eggs, beaten
¾ cup orange juice
1 teaspoon vanilla
¾ cup plain unsweetened yogurt

*Topping*
2 tablespoons grated orange peel
½ cup chopped pecans
3 tablespoons butter
3 tablespoons cane syrup or honey

Combine flour, baking powder, baking soda, cinnamon, and orange peel in a medium bowl. Stir in pecans. In a small bowl, combine eggs, orange juice, vanilla, and yogurt and add to flour mixture. Mix and pour into greased 10 x 10 baking pan. Sprinkle on orange peel and pecans.

Melt butter and blend with cane syrup. Spoon over cake batter. Bake at 375° for 45 minutes or until knife inserted in center comes out clean.

# Butter Pecan Rice

2 tablespoons butter
¾ cup chopped pecans
2 cups cooked brown rice
Salt and pepper to taste

In a 10-inch skillet melt butter. Add pecans and stir briefly, then add cooked rice. Stir and cook just long enough to heat thoroughly. Add salt and pepper to taste.

Serves 4 to 6.

My friend Gert explained that her Best Ever Pie was named when someone first tasted it and exclaimed, "This is the best pie I ever tasted." Still, I wasn't quite prepared for the response my first baking of the pie received. Rickey and I were sitting on the wood box one rainy afternoon, shelling pecans. When I mentioned that it was almost time to try Gert's recipe, I noticed that Rickey's rate of shelling accelerated.

The next day, however, we had lots of grove work to do. Summer rains had left plenty of weeds to hoe, and it was time to fertilize again. "I'm not sure I'll have time to bake the pie today," I told Rickey. "Oh, that's O.K.," he assured me. "I'll fertilize the grove while you bake the pie." And off he went without shoes over the hot sand, carrying the sacks of fertilizer under his arm.

When he was done, so was the pie, much to his relief, for he had smelled it baking all through the grove. After the first slice, and then the second, he sat on the woodbox gazing out over the grove and murmuring "best ever, best ever" until I was obliged to cut him a third piece. And I'm not sure of the fate of the slice he cut to "take home to his brother."

# Gert's Best Ever Pie

2 eggs, separated
1 cup sugar
1 teaspoon cinnamon
1 teaspoon ground cloves
½ cup chopped pecans
½ cup seedless raisins
1 tablespoon melted butter
1 tablespoon vinegar
8-inch unbaked pie crust

Preheat oven to 350°. In a medium bowl, beat egg yolks well. Sift sugar, cinnamon, and cloves and add gradually to egg yolks. Add pecans, raisins, and butter.

In a small bowl, beat egg whites well. Fold into above mixture. As you fold, add vinegar. Pour into crust and bake at 350° until crust and top are nicely browned (about 30 minutes). Don't overbake — burns easily! Cool. Whipped cream may be served with the pie.

Serves 6.

*Moonlight Oyster Roasts*

Fall is the season for oysters, which are at their peak during the "r" months, such as September, October, November, and December. I buy the oysters from the nearby Gulf fishing villages of Cedar Key and Appalachicola. Then I plan a moonlight oyster roast.

I make sure the oysters are well-chilled on ice before the first friends arrive. The full moon rises steadily over the cabbage palms, illuminating their long trunks and leaving the shaggy heads in semi-darkness. The wind through the palm fronds sounds like flowing water. We light the fire with fallen fronds which blaze up immediately; the light shines on the group, then quickly fades. The dry wood ignites and burns with help from the fronds. While waiting for a good bed of coals, some of us can't resist sampling the cold oysters with a few drops of our own Cross Creek hot pepper sauce. Others begin playing guitars and fiddles, and the moon lights up our faces as the music lightens our hearts.

# Nana's Oyster Sauce

*My red-headed grandmother made this spicy sauce for oyster cocktail. I make it for serving on raw oysters with crackers. Adjust the horseradish and hot sauce to taste, but maintain the thickness of the sauce, so plenty adheres to the oysters!*

1 cup tomato ketchup
⅓ cup prepared horseradish
½ cup lemon juice
2 teaspoons hot sauce

Combine all ingredients and chill thoroughly in refrigerator. Makes about 1¾ cups.

Oysters are steaming on the grill next to long loaves of pungent garlic bread. A finely shredded cole slaw with tart tarragon dressing is a pleasant surprise for those expecting the customary mayonnaise dressing. Kate arrives with her basket of spicy persimmon bread redolent in a blue cloth. Lanterns light the long plank tables. Orange trees glisten and their lichen-covered trunks look white in the moonlight.

# Eva's Garlic Butter

¼ pound butter, softened
1 clove garlic, crushed or finely chopped
½ teaspoon Italian seasoning herb mix

Mix butter, garlic and herbs until well blended. Use a mortar and pestle or mix by hand. Refrigerate and let flavors blend for at least 2 hours.

Good served on Cuban, Italian, or other crusty bread.

*Persimmons*

By fall, the persimmons that matured so slowly through the summer are glowing bright orange from the trees in Kate's backyard. After we've plucked nearly all the fruit from our own trees, we find other trees in the community whose owners find the orange fruit a nuisance. Some people even threaten to cut the trees down because the fallen fruit turns mushy underfoot and tempts raccoons and possums. At the first neighbor's call we initiate our "persimmon possum patrol" and fill our baskets.

When our friend Memree gets her first batch of fall persimmons, we can expect a call, "Come on over for persimmon pudding." We gladly travel the ten miles to her horse farm and up the long driveway bordered by century-old live oak trees. The sand-rutted driveway passes by grazing horses and weathered frame houses. The pudding is in the oven when we arrive, and we savor the spicy aroma while the coffee perks. Persimmon pudding is always better than we remembered because we've waited so long for this taste of fall.

## Memree's Persimmon Pudding

2 cups persimmon pulp
3 eggs, beaten
¾ cup brown sugar
½ cup melted butter
2 cups evaporated milk or light cream
1½ cups whole wheat flour
1 teaspoon baking powder
1 teaspoon baking soda
2 teaspoons cinnamon
1 teaspoon ginger
½ teaspoon allspice
½ teaspoon nutmeg
½ cup chopped pecans
½ cup raisins

Mix persimmon pulp, eggs, brown sugar, butter, and milk. In a large bowl, mix flour, baking powder, baking soda, spices, pecans, and raisins. Blend liquid and dry ingredients and pour into a greased 9 x 14 x 2 baking pan.

Bake at 325° for 1 hour or until firm.

# South Moon 'Simmon Bread

3 large Japanese persimmons (very ripe)
   (about 2 cups pulp)
2 eggs, beaten
1 cup cane syrup (or ⅔ cup brown sugar
   plus ½ cup plain yogurt)
2 cups whole wheat flour
2 cups unbleached white flour
1 teaspoon cinnamon
1 teaspoon nutmeg
½ teaspoon ginger
½ teaspoon allspice
2 teaspoons baking powder
1 cup raisins
1 cup chopped pecans

Preheat oven to 375°. With a sharp knife, remove stem end of persimmons and carefully scoop out the pulp with a spoon.

In a medium bowl, combine persimmon pulp, beaten eggs, and cane syrup. Beat until fluffy with an electric mixer or by hand.

In a large bowl, sift together the flours, spices, and baking powder. Stir in the raisins and nuts. Add the wet ingredients all at once and mix only until blended.

Pour batter into 2 greased 8 x 8 baking dishes or three 4½ x 8½ bread pans. Bake at 375° for 35 minutes or until a knife inserted in center comes out clean.

# Persimmon Meringue Pie

2 cups persimmon pulp
  (2 or 3 large persimmons)
⅓ cup honey
½ teaspoon mace
1 teaspoon grated lemon rind
⅛ teaspoon salt
3 eggs, separated
2 teaspoons butter, melted
½ cup pecans, coarsely chopped
9-inch pie shell, baked
¼ teaspoon cream of tartar
6 tablespoons sugar

Peel persimmons and press through a coarse sieve or mix in blender. Add honey, mace, lemon rind, and salt and cook slowly for 5 minutes.

Beat egg yolks; add melted butter and a small amount of cooked persimmons. Pour into persimmon mixture and cook, stirring constantly, until the mixture is slightly thickened. Fold in pecans and pour into pie shell.

Make meringue by beating egg whites with cream of tartar until soft peaks form. Then gradually beat in sugar, beating until stiff peaks form. Spread meringue over filling, being sure to cover and seal edges completely. Bake at 350° for 10 to 12 minutes or until meringue is lightly browned. Chill several hours before serving.

Serves 8.

One Christmas I decided to surprise Kate and Gary with some young persimmon trees to plant among the old ones in their yard. I drove to a nursery north of town where I met a wiry old man wandering among the persimmon trees. He was extolling the virtues of each different type. As he spoke, with eyes closed, fingers to his lips, he seemed to be tasting each flavor. "In my next reincarnation," he mused, "I believe I'll be a Chinese cultivator of persimmon orchards, discovering and blending choice varieties, attaining more wonderful and delectable fruits." Enjoying his poetic ramblings, I asked, "Why not come back as a persimmon?" There was a twinkle in his eyes. "Oh no," he said with certainty, "for then I'd get et."

### A Hankering for Greens

Along with many other Southerners, I doubt that I could live without eating greens at least once a week. There's never a question as to whether my fellow gardener Rickey and I will plant collards, or turnips, or mustard greens in the Rawlings garden. We plant them all! Just the mention of cooking a pot of greens on the woodstove sends one of us to the garden to pick a fresh "mess" of greens. We agree that we could eat greens every day, especially with hot cornbread to dunk in the "pot liquor," the broth the greens have cooked in. Rickey drinks pot liquor as an aid to longevity. His model is his grandfather, once a patriarch of the nearby black community, who drank a cup of pot liquor every day and lived to be 102.

We would grow greens year-round if we could, but the summer heat is usually too much for them. By fall, then, we experience a real hankering and are especially appreciative when the first crop is in.

# Sweet and Sour Stuffed Collard Rolls

1 dozen large collard leaves

*Filling*

2 tablespoons cooking oil

1 cup diced onion

3 cups diced turnips

3 cups diced rutabagas

½ cup sliced mushrooms

1 teaspoon each basil, thyme, and
marjoram

1 cup cooked lentils

1 cup cooked barley or rice

1 pound cooked lean ground sausage or
beef (optional)

Salt and pepper to taste

*Sweet and sour sauce*

2 tablespoons cooking oil

4 cloves garlic, minced

2 cups diced onion

4 cups diced tomato

2 tablespoons honey

2 tablespoons cider vinegar (or hot
pepper vinegar)

2 cups tomato sauce

Wash collard leaves and cut off stem ends. In large Dutch oven steam leaves over boiling water until pliable. Set aside to cool.

Heat oil in Dutch oven and saute onion, turnip, and rutabaga until tender. Add mushrooms and herbs and cook briefly. Stir in cooked lentils and barley. Add salt and pepper to taste, and mix well. Remove to large bowl to cool.

To make the sauce, cook garlic and onion in oil until golden. Add tomato, honey, vinegar, and tomato sauce. Simmer for 15 minutes.

Place ¼- to ½-cup of filling mixture in each collard leaf. Roll into a bundle, tucking in sides while rolling. Layer in large Dutch oven and cover with sweet and sour sauce. Cover and bake in 350° oven until collard rolls are tender (about 40 to 50 minutes).

Serves 4 to 5.

# Marilyn's Southern Greens and Beans

1½ cups mixed dried beans and peas
8 cups water
4 cups chopped greens — preferably a
    mixture of collard, mustard, and
    turnip greens (whatever's in the
    garden)
2 to 3 hot peppers (optional)
1 tablespoon olive oil
2 cloves garlic, minced
1 cup diced onion
3 medium tomatoes, diced
2 tablespoons chopped fresh basil
Salt and pepper to taste

Rinse beans and peas and soak overnight. Drain and place in large Dutch oven with water. Cook for 1 hour or until they begin to soften. Then add greens and cover briefly until wilted. Stir, adding more water if necessary (though not too much, for the broth should thicken as it cooks). Remove cover, add hot peppers, and continue to simmer.

In a medium saucepan, saute garlic, onion, tomatoes, and basil in olive oil until soft. Add to greens and beans and simmer for one-half hour. Salt and pepper to taste. Serve with hot pepper vinegar and cornbread.

Serves 6 to 8.

Surprise that special "someone" in your life with a sweet potato pie at his next meal. Quality sweet potatoes from South Carolina curing houses are loaded with vitamins A, B & C.

# S.C. SWEET POTATO BOARD

If your sweet tooth doesn't need satisfying, try South Carolina sweet potatoes in a variety of other ways including baked, candied, fried or whipped. Sweet potatoes are a provider of food energy so necessary during the winter months.

## SOUTH CAR SWEET POTATO PIE

1¾ cups mashed cooked South Car sweet potatoes

1 cup sugar

½ tsp. nutmeg

¼ lb. butter or margarine

1 cup cream or evaporated milk

1 egg

Put all ingredients to mixing bowl and with mixer un light and fluffy. and bake at 350°.

## Sweet Potatoes

I have a section in my recipe notebook titled "Southern," and for a long time the first recipe in it has been "sweet potato pie." Years ago my brother Doug clipped the recipe from a newspaper and sent it to me. It was in an advertisement put out by the South Carolina Sweet Potato Board. Whenever I think of this organization, I envision white-haired Southern gentlemen sedately seated at board meetings drinking coffee and sampling the sweet potato pie, all the while extolling the virtues of "quality sweet potatoes from South Carolina curing houses." The ad further described the sweet potato as a "provider of food energy so necessary during the winter months," and exhorted the reader to "surprise that special 'someone' in your life with a sweet potato pie at his next meal."

I didn't need any convincing. I'd long revered the sweet potato as one of the finest of vegetables, and the smell of sweet potatoes baking is the essence of my southern kitchen. I find them especially savory baked slowly in a wood cookstove or in the coals of an outdoor fire. Whenever I cook outdoors for guests, I can count on my friend Betty to scrutinize the coals and comment, "Looks like a 'tater fire to me."

One of my favorite breakfasts in the woods is a cup of good, strong coffee and a cold 'tater left from the previous night's cookout. Once I sent friend Hank on a plane trip north carrying a paper sack of baked sweet potatoes. After spending fall and winter at the Creek, Hank had learned to enjoy many southern specialties. However, he decided that munching on sweet potatoes on the plane while everyone else drank cocktails would be embarrassing. He reconciled the dilemma by eating his potatoes en route to the airport.

Though the South Carolina Sweet Potato Board urges cooks to use South Carolina sweet potatoes, I enjoy growing my own. The leaves are almost heart-shaped and grow on vines through the hot summer while the orange tubers mature deep in the soil. When a small patch in the Rawlings grove yielded my first good crop, I proudly pulled the vines and filled my large grapevine basket three times. I could hardly wait to taste the potatoes that evening, but I was sorely disappointed by their blandness. Ruefully, I thought of all the shovelfuls of soil I had turned and all the weeds I had pulled.

The next time I saw my neighbor Vanessy, I told her of my sorrow. A veteran farmer and long-time lover of the soil, Vanessy covers her white hair and fair skin with a broad-brim straw hat and hoes her rows barefoot just as I do. We wave from our neighboring gardens and happily go about our hoeing, sometimes stopping long enough to chat about the cucumbers or peas. This time she smiled, "Oh honey, you've got to let sweet potatoes age. Let them set for a few weeks or more and then try one. The sugars will develop and they get sweeter right along." I stored them in the pantry and, sure enough, they not only lasted for months but got better the longer they cured.

I realize most people don't share my passion for a good sweet potato, but everyone will enjoy my sweet potato pie. I make a deep-dish pie, thick and spicy, using cane syrup or honey according to the sweetness of the sweet potatoes.

# Sweet 'Tater Pie

3 cups mashed cooked sweet potatoes
⅔ cup cane syrup or honey
3 eggs, lightly beaten
1½ cups milk
1 teaspoon nutmeg
½ teaspoon salt
1 tablespoon orange juice or rum
    (optional)
½ cup chopped pecans (optional)
1 recipe 2-crust pie dough

Preheat oven to 450°. Line a 2-quart round ovenproof casserole with thinly-rolled pastry dough, or make two 9-inch pie shells.

Combine potatoes with syrup or honey. Mix thoroughly. Add eggs, milk, nutmeg, and salt. Add orange juice or rum, if desired. Pecans may be added to filling or sprinkled on top. Pour into shell.

Bake in a 450° oven for 15 minutes. Lower temperature to 325° and bake 30 minutes or until firmly set.

Serves 8.

# Sweet 'Tater Biscuits

1¾ cups unbleached white flour
½ cup whole wheat pastry flour
2 teaspoons baking powder
½ teaspoon baking soda
½ teaspoon salt
¼ cup melted butter
1 cup cooked, mashed sweet potatoes
1 tablespoon cane syrup or honey
⅔ cup milk

Preheat oven to 450°. Sift white flour and whole wheat flour together in large mixing bowl. Sift again with baking powder, baking soda, and salt.

Melt butter and add to mashed sweet potatoes. Mix in cane syrup, then milk. Beat together well.

Add sweet potato mixture to sifted ingredients. Mix thoroughly and quickly. Turn onto floured board, adding scant amounts of flour if necessary. Don't handle the dough too much. Roll or pat to ½-inch thickness. Cut into rounds with floured biscuit cutter.

Bake on greased baking sheet at 450° for about 15 minutes.

Makes approximately 15 biscuits.

Sometimes Snow and Ella May come by to advise me on the old orange grove. Both of them have lived in the area most of their lives, and Snow was Marjorie's grove foreman in the '30s. One fall day we were having a cup of coffee by the woodstove in the kitchen. When Snow noticed the largest sweet potatoes set aside in the pantry, his dark eyes lit up. "Now there's the ones you want for pies," he allowed. The next day, when the first pie was baked and still warm, I invited Snow and Ella May over. They turned the invitation around and invited me for freshly-caught "specs," cornbread, roselle jelly, garden peas, tomatoes, and pickles recently canned. We finished with sweet potato pie and coffee. Dusk entered the house as we talked quietly, and night sounds permeated the walls. A horned owl called from the magnolia overhead.

Whenever I travel the white sugar-sand road winding to Snow and Ella May's house, I look forward to their quiet companionship as much as to the good meal. I scarcely have time to park my car under the biggest magnolia I've ever seen before Ella May calls a greeting from the porch. The house sits among fruit trees with a garden clearing nearby. The woods beyond are dotted with ponds and wrap securely around the small homestead. It was here that "Miz Rawlings" first met Snow and asked him to take care of her grove. Fifty years later, he's helping me restore the grove, advising me, offering encouragement.

Jack-o-lanterns glow from the porch and greet friends coming over for a bonfire on Halloween night. I light the fire in the orange grove at dusk, and friends arrive at the appointed time of "dark-30" or later. Walking through the dark grove to the fire we wind among gnarled citrus trees. The full moon rises slowly through the shiny leaves. Kate puts a pot of mulled cider in the coals and our friend Michael brings apples from the Carolina mountains for baking in the oven.

# Mulled Cider

1 gallon natural (unpasteurized) apple
  cider
2 oranges
30 to 40 whole cloves
5 sticks cinnamon
3 cups rum

Cut oranges into ½-inch thick slices. Stud slices with cloves. Break cinnamon sticks into 1-inch pieces.

In a large pot, bring cider to boil and add orange slices and cinnamon. Reduce heat and simmer, uncovered, about 1 hour. Remove from heat and spoon out orange slices and cinnamon. Stir in rum. Serve hot.

Makes 16 1-cup servings.

*Thanksgiving*

For me, the first real feeling of fall every year comes with Thanksgiving. The air cools, and the first crop of oranges sweetens and is ready to eat. It's time to make roselle relish and to visit our neighbor, Mr. Sykes, while he boils and skims fresh cane juice into a dark syrup. Kate and I buy enough of the sweet cane syrup to last another year.

Our Thanksgiving feast is a gathering of friends and an exchange of home-harvested foods. Everyone brings his own specialties, and we spread the foods on outdoor tables under the pines at Kate and Gary's house.

# Dixie Turkey

1 12-pound turkey
½ lemon
10 cups stuffing

Wash turkey thoroughly with warm water, then dry with a cloth. Rub the turkey cavity with lemon. Fill loosely with stuffing (it will swell as it cooks). Extra stuffing may be baked separately. Secure the incision with skewers. Fill the neck cavity and close it. Tie the legs together and place turkey, breast up, in a roasting pan.

Cover the pan and roast turkey at 325° until tender (approximately 3½ hours). Baste every ½ hour with pan drippings. Remove cover for last ½ hour of cooking so the skin can get brown and crisp. When done, breast meat and leg should be tender, and legs will pull readily from the body.

Serves 12 to 15.

# Apple Onion Stuffing

½ cup butter
1 large sweet onion, chopped
1 large apple, peeled and chopped
1 cup chopped fresh parsley
2 teaspoons dried thyme
1 teaspoon dried sage
½ teaspoon dried rosemary
½ teaspoon black pepper
1 teaspoon chopped garlic
1 cup water
1 cup raisins
6 slices whole wheat bread, toasted and
    cubed
4 to 6 cups crumbled corn bread
3 cups cooked rice
1 cup chopped walnuts

In a large saucepan, melt butter. Add chopped onion, apple, parsley, herbs, pepper, and garlic and saute until onion is transparent, about 2 minutes. Add water, bring to boil and stir in raisins. Simmer about 2 minutes.

Remove from heat. Stir in bread cubes, corn bread, rice, and walnuts and mix until all ingredients are moistened, adding more water if necessary.

Makes enough stuffing for a 20-pound turkey.

# Cranberry-Orange Relish

1 bag (10 oz.) fresh cranberries
2 oranges
¾ cup orange blossom honey

Run cranberries and oranges through a food chopper using a medium blade or chop in blender or food processor until small pieces are formed.

In a medium saucepan, bring mixture to simmer and stir in honey. Simmer, uncovered, 15 to 20 minutes. Chill at least 2 hours.

Makes about 3 cups relish.

# Ted's Butter and Parsley Potatoes

12 medium new potatoes, unpeeled
4 tablespoons butter
¼ cup chopped fresh parsley
2 teaspoons chopped fresh majoram or
    1 teaspoon dried
1 large clove garlic, crushed
¼ teaspoon freshly ground black pepper
1 cup cooked diced ham (optional)

Wash potatoes and cut in quarters. Steam or boil until nearly tender. Drain.

In a 10-inch skillet, melt butter and saute parsley, marjoram and garlic until parsley is limp. Stir in potatoes and pepper and saute gently until potatoes are cooked. Stir in ham and warm through.

Serves 4.

# George's Backhand Chutney

*Originally created to bring the local ping-pong team through the first heat of a tournament, this spicy chutney became a favorite accompaniment to all our covered dish suppers.*

2 cups apple cider vinegar
2 cups honey
5 medium apples, peeled and chopped
1 lemon, thinly sliced
2 cups raisins
½ cup fresh ginger, thinly sliced
1 clove garlic, chopped or crushed
½ teaspoon cayenne pepper

Bring vinegar to a boil in a medium saucepan. Stir in honey. Add all other ingredients, reduce heat, and simmer until fruit is tender, about 20 minutes.

Follow standard canning process for storage or make smaller batch for immediate use. (Important: contact your county extension office home economist or consult USDA bulletin #92 for complete and safe canning instructions.)

Makes about 6 cups.

# Orange Rice

¼ cup butter
½ cup chopped fresh parsley
4 tablespoons grated orange rind
1½ cups orange juice
½ cup water
2 cups uncooked white rice

In a medium saucepan, melt butter. Stir in parsley, orange rind, juice, and water and bring to boil. Stir in rice. Reduce heat and simmer, covered, 25 minutes or until liquid is absorbed.

Makes 8 servings.


# Brandy Butternut Pie

2 eggs
1⅔ cups evaporated milk or light cream
2 cups cooked mashed butternut
    squash or pumpkin
⅔ cup cane syrup or ½ cup brown sugar
1½ teaspoons cinnamon
½ teaspoon nutmeg
½ teaspoon ginger
½ teaspoon allspice
½ cup brandy
Pastry for a 12-inch deep dish pie

Heat oven to 425°. Beat eggs in a medium bowl. Add milk and squash and blend well. Mix in rest of ingredients.

Pour into pie shell. Bake 15 minutes at 425°; then reduce heat to 350° and bake 35 minutes or until knife inserted in center comes out clean. Chill and serve with whipped cream flavored with brandy.

Serves 8 to 10.

# Di's Pineapple Cheese Pie

*Crust*
1¾ cups crushed graham crackers
6 tablespoons butter, melted
1 teaspoon cinnamon
1 tablespoon honey

*Filling*
2 packages (8 oz. each) cream cheese
2 eggs
½ cup honey
1 teaspoon lemon juice or vanilla
½ teaspoon salt

*Topping*
1½ cups sour cream
2 tablespoons honey
½ teaspoon vanilla
⅛ teaspoon salt
1 fresh pineapple, cut into chunks

Combine graham crackers, butter, cinnamon, and honey; pat into 9-inch pie pan. Chill. Mix cream cheese, eggs, honey, lemon juice, and salt. Pour into crust and bake at 300° for 20 minutes. Let cool at room temperature.

Mix together sour cream, honey, vanilla, and salt and pour over pie. Bake 5 minutes until glazed. Allow to cool, then top with pineapple chunks. Now the tough part: refrigerate 6 to 12 hours before serving.

Makes 8 servings.

My first fall in Cross Creek, when I was still living in Marjorie Rawlings' home, was a memorable one. By the time the wood cookstove was safe and functional it was nearly Thanksgiving. I figured that, since the house was open for visitors, why not bake and create a festive air? My folks drove the 150 miles from the small town of Frostproof to have Thanksgiving with me. I prepared the turkey with cornbread and pecan stuffing, and a slow fire in the cookstove browned it to tender perfection. Marjorie would have been proud. Turnips and greens simmered on top of the stove. As the aromas wafted through the breezeway separating the kitchen from the main house, some visitors bemoaned that they had already eaten their Thanksgiving meal. Others invited themselves to dinner!

# Indian Pumpkin Bread

2 cups pumpkin puree
¼ cup oil
½ cup cane syrup or honey
2½ cups whole wheat flour
2 teaspoons baking soda
2 teaspoons cinnamon
½ teaspoon ginger
1 cup chopped pecans

Preheat oven to 350°. Blend together pumpkin, oil, and cane syrup. In a medium bowl stir together well flour, soda, cinnamon, and ginger. Stir flour mixture into wet ingredients. Add pecans, stirring quickly, only until well-blended.

Spoon into 2 greased 8 x 4 bread pans or 2 greased 1-pound coffee cans for round loaves. Bake at 350° for 10 minutes, then 325° for 40 minutes or until done. Cool in pans for 15 minutes before turning onto a rack to finish cooling.

# Mary's Cornmeal Pecan Stuffing with Apricots

1½ cups dried apricots, soaked
    overnight, or ½ cup sliced kumquats
¼ cup butter
2 cloves garlic, minced
1 medium onion, chopped
½ cup sliced celery
1 teaspoon each nutmeg, ginger,
    paprika
½ teaspoon salt (optional)
1 teaspoon black pepper
2 cups cubed day-old bread (a mixture
    of whole wheat, unbleached, or rye)
2 cups cubed, day-old cornbread
¼ cup chopped dill and parsley, mixed
2 eggs, beaten
1½ cups chopped pecans

Soak apricots overnight. Drain and chop. Reserve liquid for moistening stuffing, if needed.

Melt butter and saute garlic, onion, and celery for 2 minutes. Remove from heat and add spices. In a large bowl combine cooked mixture with breads, dill, and parsley. Add eggs and mix well. Add apricot liquid if needed. Mix in chopped pecans and apricots.

Allow ½ cup stuffing per 1 pound of bird. Stuff bird just before roasting. Stuffing is done when it reaches an internal temperature of 165° to 170°.

Yields 5 cups.

Note. For a crisp version, bake at 350° in a greased 9 x 13 pan for about 40 minutes or until brown.

# Lemon Rice

1 cup short-grain brown rice
Peel of ½ lemon, finely grated
½ teaspoon salt (optional)
1½ cups water
½ cup lemon juice

Combine rice, lemon peel, salt, water, and lemon juice. Bring to a boil and cook for 3 minutes. Stir once or twice, then turn heat very low and cover pot tightly. Simmer for 45 minutes without lifting the lid. Remove from heat and let stand for 10 minutes.

Serves 4.

# Gramma Barnes' Steamed Indian Bread

1½ cups whole wheat flour
1 cup cornmeal
1½ teaspoons baking soda
½ teaspoon salt
½ cup molasses
1⅔ cups milk
1 cup raisins

Combine flour, cornmeal, baking soda, and salt in a large bowl. Combine molasses and milk. Add the liquids to the dry ingredients and mix well. Fold in raisins. Pour batter into 2 greased 1-pound coffee cans with tight-fitting lids. Cans should be about three-fourths full. Put lids on tightly.

Place cans on a trivet in a large pot with 1 inch of boiling water. Cover pot tightly. Boil over high heat until steam begins to escape; then lower heat and steam for 3 hours.

Remove coffee can lids (use pot holders) and allow all steam to escape before unmolding.

*Roselle*

Roselle, the Florida cranberry, is an "old-timey," domestic plant sometimes found in southern gardens, though now it has been nearly forgotten. A member of the cotton and okra families and related to the hibiscus, roselle makes a pretty ornamental bush in the yard and can grow to be six feet tall. The plant resembles okra, but instead of an edible green pod, it has a fleshy, scarlet calyx that can be used in jelly-making.

Roselle is native to India where it is grown for its fiber; it is also cultivated extensively in Australia. It was probably introduced to Florida from Jamaica and is often called "Jamaica sorrell." Other names for the plant are "jelly okra," "jelly bush," and "lemonade bush." I first read about roselle in Marjorie Rawlings' *Cross Creek Cookery*, and it was her grove caretaker, Snow and his wife Ella May who introduced me to the plant. They still grow roselle and make a clear, scarlet jelly from it.

I remember clearly the day of gathering roselle from their garden. The white sand road to their house was soft and powdery from lack of rain. Near the picnic table where we sat in the shade, there were red magnolia seeds scattered over the white sand. Ella May said, "Don't you need some roselle for your garden?" Grateful for their gift of the small heart-shaped seeds, I began to grow roselle too. It has become one of my favorites, not only because of its unusual beauty, but also for its tolerance of the summer heat.

Roselle matures around Thanksgiving, so I don't have to depend on northern cranberry bogs for Thanksgiving relish. I just take a basket to the garden and pick the fresh red calyxes. They are ready to use about three weeks after the blossom falls. I set them to simmer until tender with orange peel, then add honey, but not too much because the relish should maintain some tartness. When the mixture cools, I add pecans.

## Roselle Relish

6 cups roselle calyxes
4 cups water
1 tablespoon grated orange peel
1 cup honey, or more to taste
½ cup chopped pecans (optional)

Remove the calyxes from the central seed and stem. Wash the calyxes and place in medium saucepan with water and orange peel. Simmer until just tender (5 to 10 minutes). Do not overcook. Rub through coarse sieve and return to pan. Bring to boil and add honey to taste. Cook and stir until honey is dissolved. Add pecans when cool.

Makes about 4 cups.

The juice of roselle makes an unusual, clear red jelly, but I prefer to retain the pulp of the plant and make the rich, red jam.

# Roselle Jam

4 cups roselle calyxes
3 cups water
1 cup palmetto honey (or any light
    honey)

Remove the calyxes from the central seed and stem. Wash the calyxes and place in a medium saucepan. Add water and simmer until just tender (5 to 10 minutes). Rub through coarse sieve and return to pan. Bring to boil and add honey. Stir until honey is dissolved. Simmer until thick, stirring constantly. Follow standard canning instructions for storage, or make in small batches for immediate use. (Important: contact your county agricultural extension service or consult USDA bulletin #56 for complete and safe canning instructions.)

One cold winter it seemed that the roselle seeds had frozen in the ground, and those of us expecting young plants to sprout in the spring were disappointed. I planted my stock of stored seed and nothing happened. I called Snow and Ella May and found they were having the same problem, as were the few others who grew roselle locally. Just when I feared the Cross Creek strain of roselle would die out, two seeds germinated. They were spindly and pale, but with extra care, they matured into healthy large plants that provided a good crop for another year.

*Pie Safes*

Ever since I've known what a pie safe is, I've wanted one. Pie safes are freestanding, screened cupboards where breads and pies have an airy and safe place to cool. It's so appealing to see and smell the fresh-baked goods instead of storing them away in a cold refrigerator. Pumpkins, potatoes, and onions also store well in pie safes; pears, figs, bananas and other fruits can slow-ripen on the shelves. Of course the screens are essential in Florida to keep the bugs out — and they lend a certain mystery to the contents behind the door.

I had despaired of ever owning a pie safe because restored ones had become so expensive; the only pie safes I could afford were in terrible condition. Then one day the most ravenous of the long hungrys, my friend Sean, passed the Rawlings house in a great hurry. A large crate was tied to the roof of his '63 Rambler. I knew that he was up to something when he didn't even stop to see what the noonday meal might be. I arrived home that evening to find a pie safe in my kitchen; Sean had rebuilt it for me from the ground up. A pencil-scrawled note explained, "Of course, I expect a slice or two of the first pie placed inside." Later he tried to increase my obligation to a pie a week for the rest of his life. I could never keep up with such a demand. However, when he visits now, more than likely he'll find some home-baked goods within the secret confines of the pie safe.

# 8. Winter

Oranges were introduced to Florida by the Spanish, who planted groves of sour or wild orange trees around Orange and Lochloosa Lakes. The Indians may have roasted the sour oranges over their outdoor fires. Southern ladies gathered the oranges to make a refreshing drink for the soldiers during the Civil War. In the 1870s when "orange fever" came to this area, early settlers developed groves of sweet oranges using the sour orange rootstock. The Rawlings grove is one of these; it was probably established in the 1880s. Some of the sweet trees have reverted to their sour rootstock after being frozen below the graft during a cold winter. We leave the sour oranges interspersed among the sweet because they are so hardy and beautiful and also because they are surprisingly useful.

# Wild Orange Drink

*During the Civil War, Southern ladies gathered sour oranges to make "lemonade" for the soldiers. The unique wild flavor of the sour orange makes a thirst-quenching drink.*

1 cup sour orange juice
¼ cup cane syrup (or brown sugar
   to taste)
2 cups water
3 ice cubes

Shake orange juice, syrup, and water in quart jar with lid, or mix in blender. Add ice cubes and shake or blend again.
Serves 2.

Note: You can also squeeze the juice of one sour orange into a quart of sweet orange juice to bring out the flavor.

The sour orange fruit is as sour as a lemon, but has a distinctive flavor. It makes a good, tart marmalade, a refreshing lemonade-like drink, and a good whiskey sour; it may be added to iced tea or used to marinate or accent fish. It also provides a source of amusement for us, watching the unsuspecting orange stealer sampling his "forbidden fruit."

One still winter day, I heard a rustling in an orange tree at the far end of the grove. Someone was probably reaching the high limbs for fruit. Usually we let people take a few sweet oranges to enjoy, but this sounded like branches breaking. I decided to investigate and hurried to the tree, but the person was gone. There was a trail of orange peel along the path, then a chewed section. Then the whole sour orange was dropped in disgust!

The best use for the sour orange is in the untamed wild orange pie. Whenever I make this pie, I think of walking through dense hammock and coming upon the random wild orange trees still growing there. The leaves stand out dark green and glossy; the large fruit is orange and knobby. It sets me wondering about whether they were planted by the Spanish, the Indians, or the early white settlers.

# Wild Orange Pie

*The wild orange pie is North Florida's answer to South Florida's key lime pie.*

⅔ cup juice from wild oranges
1 tablespoon unflavored gelatin
½ cup hot water
½ cup orange blossom honey
    (or any mild honey)
1 cup lowfat cottage cheese
9-inch graham cracker pie crust

Mix wild orange juice and gelatin in blender and allow to stand a few minutes. Dissolve honey in hot water and add to juice. Blend until gelatin is dissolved. Add cottage cheese and blend until smooth and creamy.

Pour into crust. Refrigerate until firm.

Serves 6 to 8.

Note: Lemon, lime, or calamondin juice may be substituted for equally good pies.

Winter is the perfect time of the year at the Creek for walking the marsh, finding choice tangerines in the woods, and sitting nights by the fire. On cool days, the fruit hangs chilled on the trees and is especially savory after I've had a long walk or when I am relaxing by a campfire. Placing the peel on the coals perfumes the air with citrus.

It was Rickey's idea that I make a tangerine pie, something more distinctive than mere orange or lemon. Since Rickey works the garden right outside the kitchen window, he's always available for recipe testing. One day while the experimental pie was chilling in the refrigerator, a woman walked into Marjorie's kitchen and was impressed by all the activity. She lifted the heavy lid of the Dutch oven and found mustard greens simmering. "Oh," she moaned, "they aren't ready yet." Touching the lid of the gray enamel coffee pot, she wondered if coffee were brewing. I poured her a cup, and she sat heavily on the small kitchen stool willing to wait.

Rickey appeared, knowing that the pie must be well-chilled by now and anxious to sample it. I cut a few slices and, glancing at Rickey, offered one to the waiting woman. She accepted eagerly and ate her piece so quickly that Rickey and I tried not to stare in disbelief. "Now then," she commented, putting her empty plate down, "my friends will never know I had any." Getting up to leave, she dug in her purse and handed me her card. "When your cookbook's ready," she insisted, "send me a copy." Rickey grinned and cut another piece of pie.

# Tangerine Chiffon Pie

*If you don't have the delightful option of picking your own tangerines when they are at their sweetest, and are picking them instead from the supermarket shelf, just be sure they are sweet and flavorful. Obtain juice by cutting in half and squeezing as you would an orange.*

1 tablespoon gelatin
4 tablespoons cold water
4 eggs, separated
½ cup tangerine juice
4 tablespoons light honey (orange
    blossom honey preferred)
1 tablespoon grated tangerine rind
1 9-inch graham cracker crust

Soak gelatin in cold water until dissolved. Beat egg yolks until thick. Add tangerine juice and 3 tablespoons honey and mix together. Cook in double-boiler, stirring constantly until mixture is thick. Stir in gelatin and tangerine rind. Cool.

Beat 3 egg whites until they begin to peak, then add 1 tablespoon honey slowly, beating until egg whites become stiff. Fold egg whites into custard and pour into crust. Chill in refrigerator.

*Hearty Winter Soups*

Gary's wood-burning pottery kiln is fired once a year. Because the three-chambered brick oven must reach a temperature of 2300°, Gary plans the firing for winter when the weather has cooled. He spends the previous months gathering and chopping pine wood into precise lengths for stoking the oven. He molds clay into bowls, vases, pitchers, and plates and puts them on drying racks in the barn. After the pieces are dry, he stacks them in the kiln, seals the doors, and begins the fire that must last for three days and nights. The slow baking continues until the ovens reach the optimum temperature. It is the prolonged slow heat with pine wood ashes that creates the special glaze of this wood-burning method.

# Winter's Back Soup

1 tablespoon oil
1 clove garlic, minced
1 cup sliced green onion
1 medium turnip, diced
1 cup finely sliced turnip greens
6 cups water
½ cup sliced mushrooms
¼ cup Japanese bean paste (miso)
1 cup cooked barley

Heat oil in a large saucepan and saute garlic, onion, and turnip. Add water and greens. Simmer until greens are nearly tender. Add mushrooms and cook until tender. Remove 1 cup hot broth and dissolve miso in it. Return to pot and add barley. Heat thoroughly, but don't allow to boil.

Serves 4.

Friends come to help fuel the kiln and offer moral support. Every fifteen minutes, more pine must be added and the coals raked out. The large oven begins to roar, and yellow flames shoot out the chimney. People work in shifts day and night to make sure that the temperature continues to climb. While the fire is being fueled, the workers feast on hearty soups, stews, and homemade breads. When the desired temperature is finally attained, weary folks relax with one last bowl of soup or piece of bread before going home.

## Spicy Bean Soup

1 pound Great Northern beans
3 lean ham hocks
3 cups water
1 teaspoon cinnamon
½ teaspoon cloves
½ teaspoon nutmeg
½ teaspoon allspice
½ teaspoon black pepper

In a large pot, cover beans with water and bring to boil. Turn off heat and allow to stand, covered, 1 hour.

Trim extra fat from ham hocks. Drain water from beans. Add 8 cups water to pot and bring to boil. Add ham hocks and spices and simmer 2 to 3 hours or until beans are tender.

Remove ham hocks, cut meat from bones and return meat to pot. Remove 1½ cups beans and a little stock from pot. Puree in blender or mash until smooth. Stir back into soup. Heat through.

Serves 8.

# French Country Stew

1 whole chicken (approximately
   2 pounds)
4 medium potatoes, with skins, cut in
   quarters
3 medium carrots, scraped and cut in
   1-inch lengths
2 large onions, cut in eighths
2 cups fresh brussels sprouts, stems
   removed
3 tablespoons unbleached flour
1 teaspoon fresh tarragon or ½ tsp. dried
1 teaspoon fresh rosemary or ½ tsp. dried
1 teaspoon fresh thyme or ½ tsp. dried
¼ teaspoon black pepper
2 medium garlic cloves, crushed
1 tablespoon gravy enhancer or
   2 tablespoons soy sauce
¼ cup white wine

Early in the day, wash chicken and place in a 4-quart cooking pot. Add 4 cups of water and simmer, covered, until tender. Remove chicken from stock and allow to cool. Refrigerate stock until chilled and remove fat. Remove chicken from bones and cut into bite-sized pieces. Refrigerate.

About one hour before serving time, place chicken stock in cooking pot, bring to a boil and add prepared vegetables. Cover and cook over medium heat about 20 minutes or until vegetables are tender. Mix flour, herbs, and pepper with ¼ cup cold water until well blended and add to stock. Add garlic and gravy enhancer and stir over medium heat until thickened. Add chicken pieces and wine and heat through but do not boil. Serve with sourdough or French bread.

Serves 6.

# Gary's Corn Herb Loaf

4 cups unbleached white flour

4 cups whole wheat flour

2 cups cornmeal

2 tablespoons sugar

1 tablespoon salt

4 packages yeast

4 teaspoons chopped fresh oregano or
  2 tsp. dried

2 teaspoons chopped fresh basil or
  1 tsp. dried

1 clove garlic, crushed

3 cups hot water

6 tablespoons melted butter

2 egg whites

In a large bowl, sift flours together and stir in cornmeal. Combine 1½ cups with sugar, salt, yeast, and herbs.

In a small bowl, mix hot water, melted butter, and garlic. Stir into dry ingredients. With an electric mixer on medium speed, beat 2 minutes. Add 1½ cups flour mixture; beat at high speed 2 minutes. Stir in enough remaining flour to make a stiff dough. Turn out on floured board and knead until smooth and elastic, about 10 minutes.

Place dough in an oiled bowl, cover with a clean towel, and allow to rise in a warm place for 1 hour. Punch dough down. Knead 1 minute. Allow to rise again 15 minutes. Divide dough into 4 equal pieces. Form into oblong loaves and place on a greased cookie sheet. Slash tops of loaves. Cover and let rise 1 hour. Brush tops with egg whites.

Bake at 375° for 30 to 35 minutes or until loaves sound hollow when thumped. Cool on wire rack.

Makes 4 loaves.

# Green Swamp Bread

*My friends Ursula and Walter, who live in Green Swamp, make this delicious honey whole wheat bread.*

1 tablespoon yeast
4 tablespoons lukewarm water
⅔ cup dry powdered milk
2 cups lukewarm water
2 teaspoons salt (optional)
2 tablespoons honey
2 tablespoons cane syrup or molasses
2 tablespoons oil
4 to 6 cups whole wheat flour

Dissolve yeast in 4 tablespoons water and set aside. In a large bowl, dissolve milk in 2 cups water. Add salt, honey, syrup, oil, and yeast. Mix well. Add 4⅔ cups flour gradually while mixing. Turn out onto floured board and knead, adding more flour as needed. Place dough in a large oiled bowl and turn so top is greased. Cover with a towel and set in a warm place to rise until doubled in bulk, about 1 hour. Punch down. Knead another 10 minutes.

Pat into 2 greased 9 x 5 bread pans, brush top with oil, cover, and let rise for another hour. Bake at 375° for 50 to 60 minutes or until done. Makes 2 loaves.

## Christmas

Kate and Gary celebrate Christmas by inviting friends over to make hand-made ornaments for their own trees. Gaily colored Christmas lights glow through the wavy old-fashioned glass in the windows of their Victorian farmhouse. The cedar Christmas tree lends fragrance to the air already rich with the sweet smells of holiday baking. Large pottery bowls hold Memree's eggnog and Kate's Mexican hot chocolate. Wooden plates and trays are arranged with cakes, breads, cookies, and fruit.

We exchange gifts of marmalades, citrus butters, Cross Creek blend tea, fruit cakes, yeast breads, herb vinegars, homemade wines, and preserved specialties.

# Kate's Mexican Hot Chocolate

4 ounces unsweetened chocolate
4 tablespoons hot water
½ cup honey
2 teaspoons cinnamon
4 cups strong coffee
6 cups milk
2 teaspoons vanilla
6 ounces coffee liqueur
*Topping*
1 pint whipping cream
1 teaspoon cinnamon
1 ounce coffee liqueur
1 tablespoon honey
12 cinnamon sticks

In a large pot, heat chocolate and water together until chocolate is melted. Do not boil. Stir in honey and cinnamon. Stir in coffee, bring to boil and simmer over low heat 15 minutes. Stir in milk and vanilla; heat through but do not boil. Remove from heat and stir in liqueur.

In a small bowl, add 1 ounce liqueur to whipping cream and beat until stiff peaks form. Beat in cinnamon and honey.

Pour chocolate into cups and top with a dollop of whipped cream. Garnish with cinnamon sticks.

Serves 12.

# Memree's Alabama Planter's Eggnog

1 dozen eggs
2 cups sugar
½ quart dark rum
10 ounces bourbon
4 ounces brandy
1 ounce Myers Rum ("Planter's Punch")
2 quarts whole milk
Grated nutmeg

Separate eggs. Beat yolks with 1½ cups sugar. Slowly stir in spirits. Add milk. Refrigerate for 24 hours or longer.

Beat egg whites with ½ cup sugar until stiff peaks form. Fold into eggnog just before serving. Grate fresh nutmeg on top.

Makes 1 gallon. May be kept up to 2 weeks in refrigerator.

# Tropical Fruit Cake

*Kate prepares these pound-cake-like delicacies early in December for Christmas giving. They are best prepared at least 2 weeks ahead to allow the rum to thoroughly soak into the cakes.*

4 cups unbleached white flour
2 teaspoons baking powder
1⅓ cups chopped pecans
1½ cups diced dried papaya
¾ cup minced dates
2 cups light rum, divided
1⅓ cups white raisins
1 cup butter
1 cup light honey (orange blossom
   preferred)
4 eggs
1 teaspoon vanilla

Preheat oven to 350°. Sift together flour and baking powder. Stir in pecans, papaya, and dates.

In a small pan, heat ½ cup rum (do not boil) and stir in raisins. Set aside until raisins are plump.

In a medium bowl, using an electric mixer on medium speed, cream butter until light. Add honey and beat until light and fluffy. Add eggs, one at a time, beating well after each addition. Beat in vanilla.

Combine butter mixture, flour, and fruits and pour into 4 greased 3 x 6 loaf pans.

Bake at 350° for 45 minutes or until done. Cool in pans for 10 minutes. Remove to racks. While still warm, pierce tops of cakes with toothpick in random pattern. Pour 2 tablespoons rum over each cake and allow to cool thoroughly.

Place 1 cup rum in a small bowl and soak four 12 x 16-inch pieces of flannel until saturated. Wrap cakes in flannel, then in 2 layers of aluminum foil. Store in a cool, dark place. For at least 2 weeks, check every few days and moisten with rum if needed.

Makes 4 loaves.

# Gramma Barnes' Gingerbread

1½ cups whole wheat pastry flour
¼ cup brown sugar
½ teaspoon cinnamon
¼ teaspoon cloves
½ teaspoon ginger
1 egg, beaten
¼ cup melted butter
½ cup molasses
1 teaspoon baking soda
½ cup boiling water
½ cup raisins

Sift flour. Combine flour, sugar, cinnamon, cloves and ginger in a large bowl.

Combine the egg with the melted butter and molasses. Stir soda into boiling water and add to butter and egg mixture.

Add liquids to dry ingredients and beat well. Fold in raisins. Pour into an 8 x 8 baking dish and bake at 350° for 30 minutes or until a knife inserted in center comes out clean. Serve with sweetened whipped cream.

# Ambrosia

*At Christmas-time, I serve ambrosia in a dish with lemon custard topped with carambola (star fruit). Don't fret if any is left over. The flavors blend and improve with refrigeration.*

4 cups orange sections
    (preferably 2 cups navel orange,
    1 cup tangerine, 1 cup temple or
    pineapple orange)
½ cup grated fresh coconut
½ cup chopped pecans (optional)

Peel oranges and section. Remove seeds and place in medium bowl. Add coconut and pecans and mix well.

Serves 4.


# Lemon Custard

2 tablespoons butter
¼ cup honey
3 eggs, beaten
2 cups milk
3 tablespoons lemon juice
2 tablespoons finely grated lemon rind
½ teaspoon nutmeg
½ teaspoon cinnamon

Preheat oven to 325°. Melt butter in small saucepan and add honey, stirring until dissolved. Beat eggs and blend together with milk and lemon juice. Stir in honey mixture until well blended. Pour into a buttered 2-quart casserole. Sprinkle with lemon rind, nutmeg, and cinnamon. Bake at 325° over a pan of water for about 45 minutes or until done.

Serves 4.

# Strawberry Jam Cake

2 cups unbleached white flour
1 teaspoon baking powder
½ teaspoon baking soda
½ teaspoon cinnamon
2 cups grated apple
½ cup raisins
½ cup chopped walnuts
1½ cups strawberry jam or preserves
1 egg, beaten
½ cup yogurt

*Frosting*
8 ounces cream cheese
3 tablespoons strawberry jam or
    preserves

Preheat oven to 350°. In a medium bowl, sift together flour, baking powder, baking soda, and cinnamon. Mix in the grated apple, raisins, and walnuts.

In a small bowl, mix jam, egg, and yogurt and beat well. Add wet ingredients to dry and beat with a spoon until well mixed, about 1 minute.

Pour into a greased 9 x 14 x 2 pan and bake at 350° for 35 minutes or until a knife inserted in center comes out clean. Cool thoroughly.

Soften cream cheese with a wooden spoon and mix in strawberry jam until well blended. Spread on top of cooled cake. Store cake in refrigerator.

## Winter and the Grove

Though winter is welcome to our part of Florida for its cool, sunny days and the respite from humidity, those frosty January nights when the temperature drops into the lower 20s are anxious ones for citrus growers. I had my share of anxious moments during the restoration of Marjorie's orange grove, but none so unnerving as the day the bulldozer arrived to clear the long-neglected grove of its underbrush.

I had begun hoeing the remnant grove, but progress with the hand tools was slow and discouraging, and some of the heavier work was beyond me. Eventually the park service decided to bring in their heavy equipment. I was torn between relief that months of potentially back-breaking work would be accomplished in a few days, and anxiety about the damage the bulldozer might do to the remaining trees. The old trees were weak and skeletal, some dying, most struggling to survive. Many had half-decayed trunks, and I was amazed that they stood at all. Yet their limbs were strong and vital, and they continued to bear fruit. They had endured through years of cold, drought, and neglect. I had hopes that the grove might thrive once again.

Now the fate of the old citrus grove hung in balance, and unless we did the restoration carefully, we might lose it all. My fears surfaced when I heard the sound of the bulldozer starting up. I walked resolutely into the grove where my supervisor, the Major, was discussing the work to be done with the bulldozer operator, A.L. As I approached, they stopped talking. "I just wanted to say," I blurted out, "that if the bulldozing hurts any of the orange trees... well, my resignation is in my back pocket."

I stood under the old magnolia tree and watched the bulldozer crash through the underbrush, knocking over small oak trees and bushes. I could feel the earth tremble under the enormous strength of the machine, and I watched anxiously for any signs of damage to the sixty trees that remained from Marjorie's original grove. But A.L. ran the bulldozer carefully and assured me the land would heal.

White cattle egrets settled gracefully on the newly turned soil in the wake of the bulldozer and moved eagerly through the grove seeking insects. A soothing, soft rain began to fall. As the sun dropped into Orange Lake, a breeze stirred the moss-hung branches of the magnolia tree. I began to visualize how the old grove must have looked with the 30-foot trees arching their canopy over wildflowers and lush grasses.

When I learned that two of Marjorie's grove caretakers still lived in the area, I wanted to meet them and seek their advice on the grove. Yet I hesitated to encroach on their privacy. Why should they welcome a stranger into their homes? Perhaps they had been bothered enough. I finally gathered my courage and drove into Chet's driveway. "Come in. Come in," Chet's wife greeted me at the door. Chet shook my hand warmly as if we were old friends. They made me feel at home, and soon Chet had promised to come by and look at the grove with me.

Chet had been Marjorie's grove keeper for many years, as well as one of her favorite hunting and fishing companions. Now the grove was nearly gone, and there was little to show for all his hard work. He walked about the yard slowly. I could tell he'd been thinking about my questions concerning the grove and the location of the garden and chicken coop. "I can hardly recall," he began, "but the chickens was back here of the pump house. Yes, you put the garden in the right place. And she grew flowers like that, too." He pointed out two large orange trees at the edge of the yard. "I set out those trees," he remembered. "They'd be forty years old now."

Marjorie's other grove caretaker, Snow, and his wife Ella May offered to help me locate the old tree rows. As we stood in the remnant grove, it seemed open and empty, with little feeling of order or symmetry. Somehow, though, as Snow scanned back over forty years, the rows began to materialize. Within two hours, we had stakes marking the north-south and east-west diagonals of the rows. Snow explained that the old groves were spaced for mules to work between the rows. I tried to imagine the quiet hum of the plow turning the rich soil. Snow stood listening too, perhaps remembering the steady clickety-clack of Marjorie's typewriter from the front porch. Years ago, that sound carried over the stillness through the grove where Snow worked steadily all day. "There was few cars going by then," he mused, "and no airboats buzzin' and a-rearin' like now."

We transplanted thirteen trees to mark the front rows of the grove. Once they began to flourish, it was time to fill in the empty spaces. I ordered the old-fashioned varieties of Parson Brown and pineapple oranges, and a few tangerines and grapefruits. We interspersed the young trees among the old sentinels.

The next three winters were exceptionally cold, and I struggled to save the young trees. I banked insulating sand high enough to cover the grafts. A friend and I fired the grove with smudge pots and wood piles. The hot fire within the kerosene burners flickered in diamond patterns of light, and the stars in the clear sky were beautifully cold and distant. One night the trees were hit especially hard and in the next few days, the leaves turned white, curled, dried out, and crackled to the ground. In following weeks, the trees dropped all their leaves. The small, new trees looked so brown and lifeless that I had little hope. I wondered if even the old trees would survive this time. I watched and waited, and finally, one day, I saw the first green shoots on the trees; I couldn't help but grin.

As I sit by the fire, a steady rain taps on the tin roof. Now the frogs are singing flute-like. Across Lochloosa marsh, the train's whistle blows a muted, drawn-out chord. On the hearth a Homosassa orange log burns.

The citrus harvest leaves my kitchen overflowing with baskets and boxes of oranges, grapefruit, and tangerines. I let the fruit ripen on the trees into winter unless a hard freeze threatens; then it must be picked immediately. The last minute fruit picking and freeze protection for the trees prove hectic and exhausting. Sometimes I find myself back at the grove late at night. I check the sand mounds insulating the young trees and wait to see if I'll need to start the kerosene burners and wood piles. Exhorting the trees to be strong, I attempt to reassure myself that they can survive the nights' freezing cold. I play a small part among those powers of nature around me and am exhilarated by the sheer beauty of the night.

# Index